Ihab Tabbara

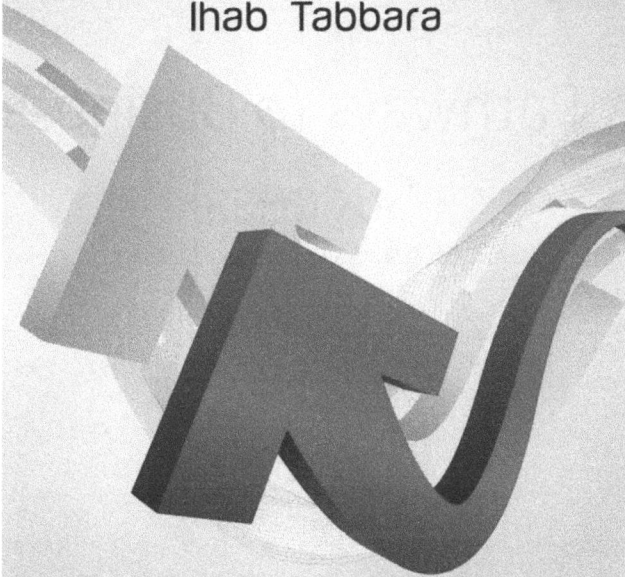

PATHWAYS TO
BUSINESS
SUCCESS

Insights and Stories to start your business

I

Pathways *to* Business Success

Insights & Stories to Start your Business

By: **Ihab Tabbara**

Copyrights © 2020

Disclaimer

The following body of work has been written as non-fiction. The events which have been portrayed by the author are expressed with the best of his knowledge and recollection. All in all, it is a peek into the author's life and the emotions associated, so there is bound to be subjectivity. It is the truth comprehended by the author and not some fiction that is made up for writing this book.

Table of Contents

Dedication

I would like to dedicate this book to my wife, my mentor and my life. Thank you for all the inspirations.

Preface

This is the success story of the author Ihab Tabbara along with key lessons and thoughts to help his readers succeed in life. The book speaks about finding yourself, building connections, taking risks and never giving up. The authors versatile life experiences all over the world have helped shape him into the man that he is today. The book takes a dive in the concept of emotional intelligence and how it effects our day to day lives. It speaks about time management, utilizing social media, and significant entrepreneurial terms and processes that can really have an impact on those seeking their dreams and desires.

This book is a must-read for anyone who is looking to develop themselves, perhaps building a brand, understanding the world from a versatile scope of view, and even people who want to read a good knowledgeable success story. The book offers some great insight in leadership qualities, how to adapt to them and become a better version of yourself, the value of constantly working on yourself and adapting to new trends and standards, all the while discussing the authors journey in life.

Chapter 1: Introduction – Who am I?

'Leadership is hard to define, and good leadership even harder.

But if you can get people to follow you to the ends of the earth,

*you are a **GREAT LEADER**.'*

*-**Indra Nooyi CEO of***

PepsiCo

My name is Ihab Tabbara, I am forty-six years old, and I am married with three children Ryan, Jade, and Lynn.

I didn't always live such a life. I have experienced a 180-degree transformation in my character from being an introvert to becoming a complete extrovert, becoming an entrepreneur, and the founder of my own consultancy firm. I have experienced a lot over my life's journey, and this book is my attempt to pass on the knowledge, wisdom, and maybe even some inspiration to my fellow readers and business owners such as yourself.

I grew up in Lebanon during the time of the civil war in Beirut, back in 1974. I belong to a wealthy family. My dad ran the family business, and I am the youngest child among my siblings. Looking back, my brother, sister, and I was rather fortunate. We lacked certain traditional family traits but were happy, for the most part. We could afford most things others around us couldn't, just because of who our parents were. Even then, I did not ask for much since I had everything I needed. I was not demanding. I was and have always been self-sufficient with my own confinement and space.

When I was four—up until I was about twelve—our parents used to send us to summer camp in Megeve, France, with our cousin for a two-month vacation. We attended a French school in Lebanon, so it wasn't out of the ordinary for us to be immersed in the French culture. We had the best time of our lives there and really enjoyed having this sort of independence. I made a lot of nice memories during that special time in my life that I still carry with me today. It also acted as a stepping stone in developing my leadership skills and in shaping my character through my life's experiences.

During my school years, I was not the brightest of students. I was a bit active and talkative in class and never focused whenever the teacher spoke. I lacked concentration. Unfortunately, at age twelve, we had to leave Lebanon because the economic and political situations had decreased significantly. So, my mum took us to Paris for a year, and then we moved to London for two years. My dad stayed behind in Lebanon to provide for us financially since his business was there. I came back to Lebanon at the age of fifteen.

I had a tough time during high school after I had moved back. I struggled with my studies and was lagging behind, so my parents had to hire special tutors who came to the house. I was even failing in some of my classes and barely made it to my graduation and final exams (French Baccalaureate). I had limited options for my undergraduate program due to my grades, so I decided to earn a Bachelor of Business Administration (BBA) at the American University of Beirut. To amuse you with my story, before I'd even joined the program, I had to do a six-month intensive English course because I had failed my IELTS exam (back then, it was called EEE).

I finally made it back to the business class but continued to struggle with my studies as I was preoccupied with my girlfriend, who is now my wife. It took me four years to graduate instead of three, like the rest of my peers.

It is safe to say that at that time, I really didn't have any goals or much of a purpose in life.

We were young and spoiled. But, maybe, it was the war that had removed all hope and ambition from young people at the time. I remember during my studies, I had suggested to my father that I wanted to do a part-time job waiter-ing at a restaurant, but he denied my request and told me that I wasn't supposed to do that kind of work.

As an adult with my nearly earned BBA, I had no idea what the heck I was going to do next. I had no experience and no valuable encounters with people in the business world, so no connections. I did not know how to talk to strangers. Fortunately, my dad had connections and contacts. He ended up speaking to my uncle, who was working in Saudi Arabia at the time. With a good word from my dad, the first job I took was as a sales rep in a building materials company—far away from my girlfriend.

I did not know how to talk to clients or even how to even approach them. It took some time and guidance from the other sales reps that I started to perform my job reasonably well. Over time, I mastered the occupation and learned how to sell and present myself. Trust me; it was not easy. That is why I am sending my eldest son, who is in his third year of studying electrical and computer engineering, to do some internship work during his undergraduate studies. I want my children to learn from my mistakes, and I strive for them to be better than I am. By the looks of it, they are lightyears ahead of me where I was their age.

I lived and worked in Saudi Arabia for a year before I decided to get married and bring my wife, Hana, to join me in Jeddah. I was twenty-four at the time, and we lived in Saudi for one year. Not long after that, the company decided to send me to Kuala Lumpur, Malaysia, to work in their affiliate branch. I guess I had done some good work during those two years as a sales rep since they decided to promote me to the position of a Sales and Marketing Manager over in K.L.

I was heading into uncharted territory; I knew no one and also didn't know the language. We landed in Kuala Lumpur looking for a house at first. We fell in love with the Asian culture, and I immediately accelerated my work process and got my feet on the ground. I got out of my comfort zone and took on a new role, along with the responsibility of managing people. It was challenging, but I did well and really enjoyed it. We had a great time during the four years living in K.L. My two sons were born there as well, and we used to travel a lot to neighbouring countries on the weekends. It was so easy to just pack our bags and take a plane to Bali, Thailand, or drive to Singapore for a couple of days.

After K.L., I had the opportunity to move again and live in Dubai, UAE working as a sales manager. We did not like it over there and only stayed for a year. That's when I told myself—and my wife—that it was time for us to start our own business and be our own boss. I was thirty years old when I decided to dive into this endeavour. So, we packed our bags and travelled home to Lebanon to start our own business together. As I mentioned earlier, we fell in love with the Asian culture, so we decided to open a small boutique selling Asian furniture and handicrafts. We operated two stores in 2002, and at the time, we travelled back and forth to Asia to buy and outsource the merchandise. The Lebanese war of 2006, however, halted our aspirations.

I had to make a tough decision and leave the business behind. Hana was going to manage what we created, and I was heading back to Saudi Arabia to work for my uncle again. But this time, with my new knowledge and experience, I took on a better role as a retail manager selling building materials. It wasn't long before I had managed to grow the business from five stores to forty stores across Saudi Arabia, Lebanon, Syria, and Egypt. I was managing 140 employees and became the General Manager of the entire company. I had a huge responsibility for the shareholders. I worked from 2006 through 2019 in this role in Saudi.

In 2016, the economy in Saudi Arabia was shaken due to the oil crisis. We had a downturn, and things were not looking good, so I decided to take advantage of this idle time and do my MBA at London Business School. I was forty-three years old, so you can imagine that I'd been away from academic studies for quite a long time. You remember how my first attempt at school went? I was afraid that I would not be accepted. But, my 20+ years of experience paid off, and I was accepted for an MBA program at a top-five university.

Oh, how the tables of fate had turned. I graduated with my MBA in July of 2019 and then decided to take a leap of faith and leave my uncle's company to start my own business. Now that I had the knowledge, the competence, and the background to do it, I entered the pathway with utmost confidence, which I had gained somewhere along the way, along with a massive amount of drive. Now I am the owner of a retail consultancy business based in Saudi Arabia and excited about the possibility of more opportunities that lay ahead in the future.

My life took a turn for the better based on the decisions I had made. In this book, I will share my wisdom, experiences, and knowledge so that you can use it as a platform for your own success. Trust me; some people don't know themselves—as much as they think they do. That is the key turning point for any transformation in life. You must understand yourself and vividly define your priorities in life so that you can succeed and be passionate about whatever you do. You have the ability to build your own identity and learn about your strengths in order to become a great leader. It all starts with you looking into the mirror and asking yourself, "Who am I?"

This book is divided into two parts, part one is about my life's journey, and the second part is about how you can reach your own pathways to business success. You can either continue reading or skip and jump straight to chapter three; the decision is yours!

Chapter 2: My Journey

My Inception

As I mentioned in my introduction, I was born and raised in Beirut, Lebanon, back in 1974. I went to a French school during my college years. I am the eldest child among my two other siblings, and our parents raised us during a tough time in Lebanon. My dad operated the family business of selling FMCG products and importing products to Lebanon from European countries to sell to the local market. The business was booming. It was very viable and generated great revenues. My grandfather passed away before I was born, so I did not have the chance to meet him. My dad had to become a father figure to his siblings; he had to take care of his six brothers and sisters. He was occupied and had a lot on his plate to handle. My dad also helped set up a separate business for each of his three brothers to run so they could be self-sufficient. He had a strong business mentality and naturally understood the different aspects of running a business successfully. He was a true entrepreneur.

He was very strict with us, but at the same time, he was very generous. He had provided us with everything we could ask for. I do not have many memories of growing up in Lebanon until the age of four. From age four onwards, our parents sent us to a summer camp in France to explore and experience a new culture. Can you imagine being four years of age and going to summer camp without your parents around to a foreign country? To most, it would seem scary, but I did not care much since I thoroughly enjoyed myself, had my brother and sister along with me. I have a lot of great memories of fun times during those months of summer camp. We used to have a lot of outdoor activities such as horseback riding, camping, hiking, ice skating, ping pong, and much more. I was very athletic and loved sports. I excelled at sports. We even had a couple of competitions among our peers, and I used to win a lot of trophies. This experience of the summer camp made me realize my passion for sports, and I'd become a big fan. We ended up going to summer camp from ages four until twelve years old. Every year it was always the same camp, and the staff and management had become familiar with us, and so they loved having us there. The Tabbara family ruled the camp in a way, and we were given special privileges and advantages among the others. I can't describe in words how great the experience was.

Let me fast forward to the age of 12. I was in eighth grade, during my school time and studying in Beirut. Unfortunately, the situation of Lebanon had gone bad, and most of the Lebanese back in 1985 had to migrate to other destinations and countries to avoid any repercussions of the terrible civil war. We decided to leave and go to Paris, France and continue our education. Of course, my dad stayed behind to run the family business; otherwise, everything would tumble down. From 1985 to 1986, we lived in Paris with my mother. Our cousins also lived there, so we had a great time with them during the weekend. We used to go to the park and play. My mom did not really enjoy living in Paris due to the language barrier. She did her best to put up with it for some time but eventually decided to move us to London, as that was where her sister was living, along with our other cousins. We stayed in London from 1986-1988. We stayed for two years and studied in a French school. I personally loved London. This is where my passion for Tennis had begun. A couple of my classmates taught me how to play the game, and I caught on quickly being an athlete. The school environment was a lot of fun, along with the people who attended along with me. Overall, it was a great experience for me.

At the beginning of 1988, things in Lebanon were a bit stabilized, so we decided to move back. I was fifteen years old. We went back to the same old school where we used to study, as I caught up with a couple of my old friends. I felt a bit bad that I had a bit of trouble remembering some of the faces and the names. That is the thing about me; my memory toward faces and names is very bad, and my friends made jokes about it. To this day, I cannot recall a name or a face if I have not seen that person for a while. Some people call it selective memory!

In the summer of 1988, Lebanon experienced another civil war. During this time, I remember spending many nights in the basement of our building. It was scary hearing bombs explode around as people died right in front of our eyes. Some of the deceased were my friends. The war ended after a couple of months, and we resumed our studies in the new term of 1989. There was much instability and shifting in our lives, but I finished the twelfth standard. Between the tenth and twelfth grade, I was quite the attraction in my school when it came to sports and girls. I was quite charming but at the same time, a very shy person. I did not know how to approach girls and date them. My mind was pretty much occupied with enjoying myself rather than my studies. I had a couple of challenges in a few classes, and my parents had to bring in a private tutor to make up for it so that I did not fail my classes.

During exam time, I used to get anxious and stressed quite often. My worst day was my final French Baccalaureate exam in twelfth grade (it is a French system). If you failed, you must re-do your whole year. It is the worst memory of my life since I barely made it through. I had what some might call a second chance, as I had failed two courses before this. Luckily, I passed, and the nightmare was over, at least for the time being.

I was eighteen years of age, having meagrely graduated from high school with embarrassing grades. What were my options for undergraduate study with my lousy grades? The only two options for me were to attend the American University of Beirut or travel to the United States. Back then, we did not have the option of applying for universities online. Everything was done through the mail. I had applied to one university there and was accepted to study electronic engineering, or something close to it. At the same time, I was accepted to the AUB to study for a Bachelor of business administration. For me to go to the USA, I needed to apply for an F1 student visa. Unfortunately, the American embassy in Lebanon was closed due to the ongoing political issues. The only option for me was to travel to Cyprus and apply there. I booked my plane and went there for a couple of days. Again, I went into an uncharted country all by myself at the age of 18. I can say that the combination of experiences in the summer camp,

Paris, and London had given me self-autonomy and independence. I figured out where the embassy was, as in those days, there were no smartphones, Google maps, nothing. You had to find your path the old-fashioned way, calling and asking for directions. Anyhow, I finally made it to the embassy and got my F1 student visa. I was super excited as I now had the option of AUB or the U.S. University, which I can't recall the name of.

I did not end up going to the U.S, and the reason I did not go was that I was dating the girl who would later become my wife. I was in love with her. I stayed behind and enrolled at AUB. The lesson I am trying to explain here is, enjoy every minute of childhood, because it is the fun part of your life. Leave the rest to destiny or fate, and you will make it through. Don't be tough on yourself; embrace every moment. Go out, enjoy yourself, and participate in sports, because it is important to keep your health and balance in check. Don't be afraid to take a risk, explore new things, and be curious. Don't depend too much on your parents and do your best to be self-sufficient.

The summer of Romance

A new journey had begun during my undergraduate years at AUB. But before I dwell on it, let me tell you the story of how I met Hana. We met during one of those summer vacations. We had casually met at a mutual friend's house, and at first, did not really hit it off. The next year in summer, we met again, and this time we did hit it off. Could it be destiny? The funny thing is that both of us did not remember having met or seen each other before. It is our common friend who told us the story, and we were both in shock and laughing at the same time. I wondered, was it meant to be? There's only a year's age difference between Hana and me. She had studied in Paris for most of her life and had decided to move to Lebanon and study Economics at a French university there. During my first year of studies, as mentioned before, I had to take a six-month intensive English class before I could join the program. I was studying like crazy just to make sure I passed so that I could begin my BBA. Again, I was lucky and ended up doing well on my final exam.

This whole system of American studies with multiple choice questions was all new for me since I had been in a French system with a different teaching method. I had to adapt, so I struggled a bit at the beginning before getting good at it. Again, during my study, I failed at one of my core classes, Macro-economics, which I hate to this day. That course had made me drop out of business school until I could get higher grades and join again. I stepped up my game and re-enrolled in the same school. I knew what the system was now, and I brought up my grades.

This whole AUB & undergraduate experience took me four years to graduate, where any other normal student would take only three years. You must put into perceptive that I was dating my wife, and we used to spend a lot of time together. Most of my time was at her university campus. I became friends with her friends, yet I did not make any friends at AUB (which does not make any sense), because the purpose for studying is also networking and making connections for future work opportunities. Again, I was not focused in life, or cared much about the materialistic values since we got everything we wanted from our parents. The family business was there, so I could join my dad for work. I had no ambition or dream to do something else. Could I have been a spoiled kid? I don't think so. Knowing myself, I was quite a humble and down to earth person. I even told my dad that I wanted to do a part-time job during my study and be a waiter at a restaurant so that I can get familiar with the business and client environment. Eventually, he turned me down and told me not to do it because I did not need to work. To be frank, I was a bit desirous of my friends who were doing some part-time jobs. Seemed like an adventurous opportunity at the time.

Finally, I graduated with my BBA in 1996. I remembered my wife joined me for the celebration, and we had taken pictures together as a souvenir with our analogue camera. I am telling you this now because later in the following chapters, you will understand the irony of the story. I will keep it a surprise for now. I want to add a note here that although my friends and brother advised me to do my MBA after a couple of years of work experience, I told myself that I was not up to the standard and that I wouldn't be able to do it as I had to pass the GMAT exam. It was a requirement, and I needed a minimum score of 650 to be accepted into a great business school. I am not the academic type, so I decided to just ignore it.

Now that I had my BBA degree in my hand, it was time for me to hit the business world. What shall I do, I asked myself? I was lost, in love, with no ambitions and dreams. Shall I join my dad's family business? What is my next move? Well, if you guessed I would go to work with my father, you guessed wrong. The moral of my lesson is that you need to embrace and trust yourself to succeed. Put in the effort and time, be dedicated to your study and never ever give up. You need to focus on your priorities in life and set goals and targets to reach. Plan your life and have ambitions; know what you want to do in the near future. Have short, intermediate, and long term goals. I wish I had a coach or a mentor to guide me through this process during my undergraduate.

Debuting Life

I am now twenty-two years of age with my BBA, and totally in love with my girlfriend. We had been dating for almost four years now. What's next for me? What should I do now, and where should I work? Shall I join the family business? Shall I look for jobs in Lebanon or outside of Lebanon? What I love about my dad is that he does not want me to join the family business, because as you may know, in most family businesses, cousins tend to get into fights, and eventually, no one speaks to anyone anymore. I guess he learned from his previous mistakes and did not want me to get caught in the same trap that he did. He told me to go and be myself and exploring new opportunities.

My dad reached out to his wife's brother, who had been living and working in Saudi Arabia for more than twenty years. My uncle had built an empire over there in the construction industry. He had been building this empire since 1980 and is a true entrepreneur and leader. He runs multiple companies in separate divisions such as construction, manufacturing, and trading, all serving the construction industry. He has even scaled it up to operate in different regions in GCC, Asia, and Africa. He has explained to me that if you need to get things done by yourself, you need to build a trustworthy team to work around you in order to expand efficiently. If you want to achieve things by yourself, you need to be fully dedicated and give 100 % to the job at hand. You need to be persistent in what you are doing and be at the right moment and time to grasp an opportunity. You also need to take calculated risks in your life and try to cope with it and manage your expectations.

Sometimes you will succeed, and sometimes you will fail. Failure will make you stronger as you learn from your mistakes, and the only way to succeed is to persevere and get back on track. At that time, this wisdom and inspiration did not make sense and did not add up since I was young and had no experience. His name is very popular and famous in Saudi Arabia. It is like saying 'Steve jobs' or any other related entrepreneurial person. He ended up offering me a job as a sales representative in one of his subsidiaries, selling building materials to construction sites. I worked there for two years, from 1996-1998.

Let me now give you some background information, both about Saudi Arabia and on my personal stuff.

Personal:

Let me tell you a funny story about my first experience and encounter at Jeddah Airport. When I entered the airport, back in 1996, there used to be huge waiting lines to get your passport stamp, and luggage was checked manually by an immigration officer. It was a nightmare. I remember I brought my whole music collection on a CD's format (I don't know if some of you remember that). I had with me fifty C.D.s, and I remember they had taken two from me: one of them was Guns n Roses and the other one was a Michael Jackson album. I couldn't figure out why they had taken those two out. I still do not understand to this day. Maybe they had good taste in music.

Back in 1996, Saudi Arabia was still under development. Roads and infrastructure were very bad, and there was no telephone line in the house. It was like a huge empty desert, and you had very limited options for social gatherings since there were no movie theatres or other fun things to do. When people came to Saudi Arabia for the first time, they would instantly get a cultural shock. How can it be one of the richest countries in the world with the biggest oil deposits and a GDP per capita of 8,300 USD yet have such poor infrastructure and living standards? I was going to the beach on Fridays and going to work during the weekdays. Life was a bit empty. Even going to a restaurant was not enjoyable at all since you had family and single men's section (what's up with that?) As a man living alone in Saudi, it is not fun at all, and I would imagine for a woman it must be even harder since they cannot drive or go out freely of their houses. I remember it was even a hassle to make international calls to speak to Hana. I had to go to a telephone booth and wait in line to make a call. Not fun at all.

Saudi Arabia / GDP per capita (1996)

8,335.80 USD (1996)

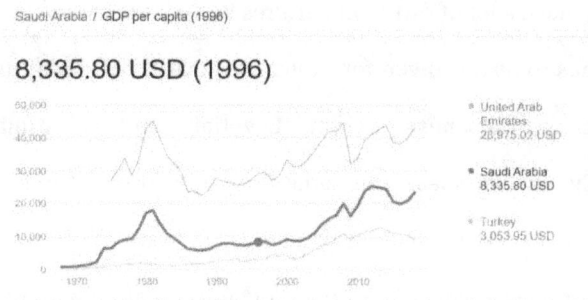

'GPD/ capita comparison among other counties (Source World Bank)'

Work:

As I have mentioned to you earlier, I was a shy person with no experience. I did not know how to talk to or approach clients. Being in sales is all about leveraging customer relationships to generate sales ad revenue. I still remember the first time I visited a construction site. I had to look for the right person to talk to and propose our materials to him. It was a rough time; my face was always turning red, words would not come out easy, and I was shaking and scared. Luckily, I had one of my supervisors guiding me and helping me secure new clients. It took me a couple of trials and along with learning and adapting to this new environment.

One point I would like to add is that in Saudi Arabia, you have a lot of different cultures in their workforce, from Arabs to Asians. Even for Arabs, we have different cultures such as Lebanese, Syrian, Egyptian, and Palestinian; although we speak the same language, the cultures are rather different. Let us also not dwell in Asian cultures from Pakistani to Indian to Filipino. I guess one of my strengths is that I am very sociable, and I can adapt to different cultures quickly and efficiently. I am like a chameleon, blending in with new environments. I learned to enjoy the experience of selling and approaching clients. It wasn't long before I got the hang of it and was getting good at it. I managed to double my sales in the span of a year and was quick to learn new things. What it takes is mostly practice and self-confidence.

The lesson I would like to highlight here is to take risks and be adventurous. Be resilient to change and embrace it. If you are at the beginning of your work-life journey, you need to explore and be confident. You have nothing to lose and everything to gain. As Steve Jobs famously said, *'Don't wait! Do something when you are young when you have nothing to lose, and keep that in mind.'*

My Second Journey

To recap, back in 1996, I was already in love with my girlfriend. We decided to get married so that she could come and join me in Saudi Arabia. One thing you need to know is that there was no tourist visa for KSA at the time, and women could not travel alone to Saudi without either being married or living with her family. A quick note: a minor percentage of women were working back then. So, you can imagine the working environment without a strong female presence. It is not pleasant at all, just a bunch of men around you. One thing I must mention about Hana is that she was always there for me to comfort me and to take care of me. She understood my whole life and childhood and is an amazing woman. She was very supportive, and we had great telepathy together. She graduated with her Bachelor of Economics and was planning to go for her Master's in Economics in Paris at Assas University. We decided to tie the knot on November 14th, 1997. I was twenty-four years of age, and she was twenty-three. Was it faith or craziness to get married so young? Maybe a little of both.

Honeymoon

I flew back to Lebanon from Jeddah a couple of days early to arrange the wedding ceremony. We also needed to prepare for our honeymoon. We had a destination in mind, we wanted to fly to the Bahamas and to the USA, but unfortunately, my visa got rejected at the embassy because of my previous F1 visa that had gone unused. On a side note, Hana is a French/ Lebanese's national, and so she had no problem with the visa issue. We did not plan for the honeymoon. I had my French visa stamped on my Lebanese passport, so we decided to go there and plan accordingly. We arrived in Paris on the 19th of November. We stayed a couple of days at her brother's house so we could plan and organize our trip. Let me lay down our honeymoon trip plan. The honeymoon was one of the most amazing and longest trips we had ever been on. The Trip consisted of a total of forty days. I guess the standard for a honeymoon is thirty, but we extended it. We were crazy!

Trip 1 – We rented a car and drove all the way to Lyon (saw an old friend of ours) and then to Megeve, where

I had gone to summer camp as a kid. We spent two nights there.

Trip 2 – From Megeve, we decided to go to Austria. We arrived at the border, and the immigration officer told me that I could not enter because Austria is not under the Schengen visa. We had driven there for nothing and had to return back. It was only a matter of a week of difference for the matter.

Trip 3- We returned to our base in Paris and took a plane to Reunion Island (a French colony). We spent a week there under the warm sun.

Trip 4 – Destination Seychelles Island. Oh my God, it was so beautiful, I can't quite put it into words. We stayed on two-islands Praslin and La Digue. We spent around 10 days there. Two love birds by a blue crystal ocean.

Trip 5 – Back to Paris from Seychelles with a ten-hour flight. We took the train and went to Vienna, Austria again. We made it this time. From tropical weather to country cold. How cool is that! We spent a couple of days in the nice cold weather and stopped every five minutes at a coffee shop for a hot chocolate with whipped cream. Of course, there was also a lot of sightseeing and museum visits.

Trip 6 – Destination: Venice, Italy. The most romantic place for tourists. Riding the gondola and going to St Mark's Square. We had to stay in a terrible hotel due to our limited budget. The toilet was not even in the room. We still had a great time, though.

Finally, we made it back to Beirut, Lebanon, after a long beautiful, adventurous honeymoon. I left Hana behind and went back to work in Saudi. I found out my general manager was looking for me due to my long absence. I had to come up with a ''bullshit'' excuse as to why I delayed my whole trip. Now, I needed to get my wife a residency permit so that she could join me in Saudi. It took a month, and she finally arrived.

The next challenge was to get her a part-time job so that she would not feel alone all day waiting for me to come back from work. As mentioned before, women cannot go outside freely from their houses. They can't drive, and plus it is difficult to grab a taxi; they are stuck in the house most of the day waiting for their husband to come back. How ridiculous is that? What kind of life is that? She landed a part-time job at the French school as a substitute teacher for a month teaching math to fifteen-year-olds. She was twenty-four, teaching children (laugh out loud) with permanent employment at the French embassy.

Married life was beautiful for both of us. We both were working and busy. At night, we used to hang out at our friends' place and stay until dawn. One thing about Saudi Arabia is that the supermarket and fast-food chains are open 24/7. People love to go out at night since, during the day, it is forty degree Celsius most of the time, over 365 days of the year. Workwise, things were good. I was the nephew of the boss, so the employees respected me, and some of them used to fear me or fear I could take over their job. Lesson learned here, if you are simply in LOVE, just travel to the moon and come back. It is the best time of your life, so cherish every moment of it. You can only do it once.

Muddy Confluence

From 1996 to 1998, I was living in Saudi Arabia, and a portion of the time I spent living with my wife. A new opportunity had arisen, and the upper management had decided to give me a chance. The chance to create a better life. I got promoted to go and work in Kuala Lumpur,

Malaysia, as a Sales & Marketing Manager in our affiliated offices, in the same industry of building materials. Hana and I moved to K.L. in the summer of 1998. The first thing we did was look for a nice apartment to reside in, preferably close to our office. Since the traffic in K.L. is such a mess, I did not want to spend my time in a car constantly stuck in traffic. Our house and office were in a very prime location near the landmark of the Petronas Twin Towers. We were young and innocent at that time. We needed to learn about the culture, visit tourist places, and make some new friends. We did a lot of sightseeing during the weekends and became friends with the French community there.

'Kuala Lumpur City tour and Tourist Attraction area.'

I quickly settled into my work. I met the team while learning how to adapt to this culture. As I mentioned previously, I am a chameleon and can easily blend among people due to my charm and charisma. Brief background history of K.L.: there are three different types of people and culture over there, and they all speak a second language, which is English. K.L. was just coming out of an economic crisis at the time. You have the Malay (we called them 'Bumi'). They are originally from the Arab world and are Muslim. You have the Indian, who have migrated a long time ago from India and are from different religious backgrounds, i.e., Hindu, Buddhist, Christian, and Muslim. Lastly, you have the Chinese, who also have different beliefs. All those three cultures have lived in harmony for ages, which is quite fascinating for me since, in Lebanon, we have a huge problem due to religious divisions and sects. This is probably a major contributor to the thirty plus year war still going on in the country today.

Over a couple of months, I got the hang of living and driving in K.L. We still did not have mobile phones back then and no google maps, so it was quite challenging. I fell in love with Asian culture. I was approaching clients easily and with confidence. I built a sales team at work around me to increase our revenue and was also training them in the new product range that I had developed in the company.

Since I had two years of building materials experience in Saudi, I had integrated this knowledge and transferred it to K.L.'s sales team.

Let me walk you through my orientation and work process and how I started:

Step 1: I introduced myself to the team and got to know them on a personal level in order to create a bond and a relationship.

Step2: Made site visits with them, met their clients, and understand what the market requirements were. Sort of market analysis on the industry.

Step 3: Identify the product range that we need to sell and make a market price survey to make sure that those products are viable.

Step 4: Outsource and negotiate with suppliers for payment terms and delivery processes.

Step 5: Promote and coach employees for the list of products to cross-sell to their existing clients.

Step 6: Allocate KPIs for each salesperson with a yearly target.

Step 7: Monitor and supervise the sales team.

Step 8: Evaluate after six months and adjust accordingly.

I was super dedicated at work. I gave one hundred percent in order to get the job done. Failure was not an option for me since I was given a challenge and needed to prove myself to the higher management and my uncle that I was worth it. Putting it all into context, with a cultural background difference, new environment, and new procedures, I have managed to embrace all of it and turn things to my advantage. I spent two years from 1998 to 2000 (Millennium era) working hard, almost like a workaholic.

On a personal level, we were having a blast; my wife and I. Still in the honeymoon stage. We enjoyed meeting friends, hanging out, going out to restaurants, exploring neighbouring countries, travelling to Thailand, Bali, and Singapore. We did not miss the chance on any public holidays to jump onto a plane. Something has always attracted us to the Asian culture. We started exploring and buying Asian antique furniture, Buddhas, handicrafts, painting, and cutlery. There were many things that really were beautifully handmade. We decorated and furnished our house with different Asian pieces. It was like you were entering into an Asian Museum. The lesson learned here is that you need to be agile, tolerant, resilient, and lead by example. Be creative and explore things as well as be open to new ideas.

Dragon Boy

Our son Ryan was born on 16th Feb 2000. We called him the Dragon boy, according to the Chinese Horoscope. I was twenty-six & my wife twenty-five. We were kids having a kid (laughing out loud). We did not know anything about raising a child, plus we did not have any help from my mother or even my mother in law since we were living far away and on another continent. I really enjoyed this parenthood experience with my first-born son. I used to give him baths, feed him, change his diaper, and even stay up all night to take care of him while he was crying. Let me put this into context for you. In Arab culture, there tend to be many nannies. I myself had one in my parents' home. This whole "taking care of a kid," thing was new to us.

We chose to name our son Ryan. As kids ourselves, we used to take Ryan everywhere with us while we travelled. Just packed the bags, jumped on to a plane, and go to a nearby destination. We were easy going and handled any situation that arose; we managed child emergencies with ease. Ryan was quite an active kid, so I had my hands full with him. I had no time to sleep, which affected my work a bit, or even going out to restaurants was affected. I could not finish my meal since I had to watch him as he jumped outside the stroller, randomly running away. Of course, we had our French friends who also had kids the same age as Ryan, so we used to have a play day for the kids. Life was beautiful, and we used to take him to the park right in front of our house, where we went almost daily. We even taught him how to swim at age one and a half with a private instructor. (We had a pool down in the apartment of the building; they call it a Condominium in K.L.).

Work in K.L. was becoming more and more challenging. The company had some financial concerns and cash flow issues. It was tough to buy materials and sell them back to the market. The top management did not want to invest money in K.L. since they believed that it was an unstable market. We had to find a solution to our problems. Such situations can either break a man or make him. Knowing how to manage money, how to handle employees and suppliers at work, and how to save money at home. At the same time, it was demotivating because you would feel that you couldn't grow within the company. At one point, we had some delayed salaries, which hit me hard and affected the house balance condition. You are living in a strange country with no close family around you and with literally no money. How can one be expected to survive? I was living in debt with my credit card, which luckily, I had two to three of. We were barely making ends meet, and it was becoming tougher and tougher on us as a couple with a baby. During those times, Hana and I argued a lot. There was no real option for me to look for work in K.L. being a foreigner. Plus, how could I leave my uncle and disappoint him like that? I had not even mentioned our money problems to him since I thought it would be unethical to tell him as he was not my direct boss. As a person, I have strong integrity and abide by my own rule of being honest, loyal, and code of ethics. I don't like to jump above my boss. I follow the rules, and I consider myself the same as a typical employee.

I think that was one of my mistakes in life. Why should I consider myself a typical employee? I should have used this to my advantage. In life, you always have the option to learn from your mistakes, and you try to work on them as much as you can. Why should a person suffer on behalf of another's mistakes? It is a choice that you make, and you must live with it. Either you keep the job or just quit. There is no right or wrong answer here. Follow your gut feeling, and think of you and your family's interest. Don't always think of others around you and what they think of you. One of the main problems of my character is that I care too much about what people think of me and care about their feelings. It is a sort of empathy, I guess.

The lesson here to learn is, don't wait for things to tremble, but take immediate action, 'a la carpe diem.' Regardless of the circumstance or the outcome, your choice will always be better than any other choice. I always say that it is better to make a choice or no choice at all. A famous quote by Deepak Chopra: "No matter what the situation, remind yourself, "I have a choice" because that takes guts, and not everyone has it.

My third path & our new treasure
Fast forward to 2002, and the work situation was getting worse every month. Salaries were delayed for almost six months now, and we were barely surviving. I decided to make my move and started to look for a job. I left

Hana for two months alone with Ryan, and pregnant again with a new baby boy in K.L. I landed in Dubai, UAE, where I had a few of my friends and connections to help me with job hunting and a place to stay. I was applying daily for a job through the Internet. It was all new for me, the online application process. There were a couple of big job platforms back then, such as Monster and Bayt.com. Those two were familiar and popular. At the same time, you had the old fashion newspaper ads. I was applying left and right with no exception.

I was even dropping by the recruiter's office unannounced. I had no choice; I needed to show my face and be visible to get some attention. Eventually, from word of mouth, I landed an interview with the biggest trading building material company in UAE. The interview was with the owner/ CEO.

As usual, I went early to the interview (I am quite time-management-oriented), and I waited for the higher management to call me in. I waited for almost two hours like a nobody, and it was very disrespectful. I was stressed, anxious, and nervous. Could it have been a tactic to throw me off? I went inside the room, and the meeting went horribly. The CEO started to harass me with questions, why me?! What is your advantage? Blah blah, you know the drill. I left the meeting face red and frustrated. I had never landed an interview before in my life that I was not prepared for.

A few days later, they called me and told me that I got the job. Surprise right! If you think about it, it is when I do not perform well in an interview, and I don't feel at ease that people want to hire me. I will take you back to it later, and you will understand why it makes sense now in my head. Was it perhaps a coincidence? Only God Knows!

They sent me the job offer, and I told them that I would get back to them and start working in a month or two. I would bring the whole family from Malaysia, and so I needed to adjust to my current situation and join them. Now, the fun part began. I went back to K.L. and told my direct boss and the CEO that I am leaving my job and going to settle in Dubai since I had a job offer.

They were a bit surprised that I was going to leave them and, at the same time, intrigued. Why is Ihab going to our competition!? By the way, the company I worked for also has offices in Dubai. So, what they did was offer me a job with better salary conditions than I had as a General Manager of the UAE operation.

They had an empty spot and needed to fill it. Who else can we give it to other than Ihab, the owner's nephew, someone that we trust and can rely on? Anyway, I was excited.

Now, I had two options in hand: a) a new challenge and a new company culture, or b) the same company with a better role and mundane responsibility? I guess I took the wrong door in my life. I choose 'b' the easiest choice. No hassle, I knew the environment and that I had the advantage to grow in the company faster. I still wonder if I had chosen the door 'a' what would have happened in my career path. Where would I be today? I guess no one has this answer for you except that it is faith and that destiny that matters.

My wife was excited to get out of this horrible nightmare but sad to leave K.L. and Asia behind. I was not much attached to the city I felt and did not have as many sentimental things, such as my wife, I guess. Hana was pregnant and in the latest stage of delivery. We waited for our new son Jade to be born on August 17th, 2002.

It was a total mess because we left our house to settle in a hotel temporarily since we were leaving Malaysia. To be frank, we did not pay too much attention to Jade since our minds were pretty much occupied with all the commotion going on around us. We waited a month after the delivery to take a plane and fly out. My wife went back to Lebanon with the kids while I went to Dubai to settle in and look for a new house. Eventually, she came and joined me with the kids after a month or two, and we were all back together as a family.

The biggest surprise here is that I found out they had hired a General Manager before me, and I was appointed as a Sale Manager. Shocking right? The CEO had screwed me over, and I was, of course, not happy about it. You can imagine how I must have felt back then: demotivated, lied to, and on top of that, I was related to the owner.

What should I do? Stay or not stay? I did not want to do the same job all over again. Visit construction sites, pitch products, and make sales.

I wanted something different and interesting. I was bored with this job. I did not have any passion or motivation anymore. Moneywise, we were just making ends meet since we now had a bigger family. Ryan started school, so we did not have an easy option to just leave things behind. We told ourselves, let us give this a try and stay behind to see where the journey will take us.

The lesson here would be not to trust anyone besides yourself. Do not be fooled by appearance and fancy talk and make sure to get a signed contract/agreement.

Path to our first endeavour

"If you have the courage to begin, you have the courage to succeed."

-Dreamquote.com

From what you have read so far, you've seen quite a bit of my history and my journey. In this chapter, I will tell you about the new beginning of my life and my career. Buckle up.

We ended up staying in Dubai for a year, and we decided that it was not enough and not even worth living there since we were not saving any money. Most people expatriate to make and save some money, otherwise what is the point? Again, Hana was pregnant with a baby girl. So, I believe this was most likely a sign for us to quit and start our lives over from scratch. We had been through our fair share of ups and downs; what worse could possibly happen? We were both resilient and loved an adventure. We have always had a strong bond and a connection. We have telepathy, understanding, caring, devotion, dedication, endurance, and pure love.

As I mentioned before, we fell in love with the Asian Culture. We asked ourselves, why don't we take this culture and implement it in Beirut, Lebanon, our hometown? We had knowledge of the industry about what to buy and where to buy it from. We had one part of the equation figured out, and the rest was to understand if the product was viable in Lebanon and that consumers will buy this kind of furniture, to begin with. We found out eventually that there were two or three boutique shops selling Asian furniture. We made an assumption that there was a demand to penetrate the market. We had the upper hand since we knew how and what to outsource, along with the experience of their culture from living in Malaysia. We had a history compared to our competitors who had never lived in Asia. We took it as an advantage and built our business model around it (well, actually, a business model is a big word since I was not an expert in entrepreneurship back then.)

I was thirty years of age, full of confidence with not a worry in the world. Of course, my dad initially helped me with the capital expenditure to get a strong start and purchase some merchandise. We left Dubai to settle in Beirut and start our own venture and company. I can now call myself an entrepreneur/business owner. Our new baby 'Asean Art' was born in November 2003. That is our brand name, by the way.

Below are the 10 Zen steps and guideline on how I did it:

Step 1: Establish a company and create a brand identity.

Step 2: Locate a prime showroom location since you are selling a niche-specific product.

Step 3: Refurbish and decorate the showroom to have an Asian cultural feeling.

Step 4: Hire three employees.

Step 5: Outsource and negotiate with suppliers for the products.

Step 6: Merchandize the products once they arrive.

Step 7: Price tag the product. Hence you need to make a market analysis and check your competitor's prices.

Step 8: Grand opening day and invite the media along with some guests.

Step 9: Manage the operation, finances, and customers.

Step 10: Evaluate and monitor.

Since it was a start-up, Hana and I were working twenty-four seven in the showroom and trying to minimize our expenses as much as possible. We did not hire a showroom manager; I oversaw the whole operation from merchandising, accounting administration, and my wife was taking care of product selection and customer relationships. We were excited, but it was very challenging. We had a responsibility towards the stakeholders. We were in charge and needed to manage our cash flow to keep the business sustainable. It was a hectic couple of months, jumping from one place to another, flying to Asia, opening in the morning & closing the showrooms at night time. We were all over the place.

I learned something new related to marketing and customer retention. We ran a couple of ad campaigns and participated in exhibitions. It was a new dimension and perception to take in control. You are the boss now, and your employees were waiting for instructions and direction.

You need to be sharp & alert all the time and to have all the answers ready. That is not an easy task at all. Be sharp, pro-active, and hungry for success. Explore and venture into the unknown by taking a calculated risk and analyse. That is my lesson for the day!

A famous quote from Jay Z,' I'm hungry for knowledge. The whole thing is to learn every day, to get brighter and brighter.

A New Blessing

Lynn, our daughter, was born on the 31st of January 2004. It was a game-changer for us compared to raising boys. It was totally a new experience for us as parents. It is a blessing to have a girl. I managed to grow the business and open another showroom in a different location to capture market shares and be at the reach of the consumers after a year. The business was growing month by month, which is why we were able to afford to spend and scale geographically in Lebanon. We used to travel back and forth to Asia to buy new merchandise and to handpick each unique piece. As I mentioned previously, our targeted customers are in a niche market, and our products were exclusive pieces of art with some background history.

Every piece we were selling had a story behind it, including the origin, the year it was made, when it was handcrafted, and the materials used. We had very limited editions of each piece, and that's what differentiated us from the competitors. It added and created value for us. We had product knowledge, having lived in Asia, and we understood consumer behaviour and what they were looking for. We needed to fill both the supply and demand sides of the equation; otherwise, our business model would not have worked out. We had to give a value proposition to our targeted customers to justify the price as well as the brand image.

My experience and knowledge of the business had opened a new door for me to explore. I started becoming creative in marketing. It really opened my eyes and allowed me to think outside the box. I remembered reading the book 'Blue Ocean Strategy' by Renée Mauborgne and W. Chan Kim, 2004. It stated the new value curve of your existing business model. How can you stand out from your competition and provide extra value to disrupt the industry? Think outside the box and be a risk-taker. Do not be afraid to explore and experiment. We started importing some gifts for corporate companies, Asian style: photo albums made from banana leaves, coconut shells, and orchid candles. Only selective products could generate more growth and business for us. We had a growing business and good times throughout the year.

As you may know, Lebanon's economic situation has been unstable for quite some time now. Unfortunately, in February 2005, our prime minister was assassinated on Valentine's Day (the irony). The country went into shock and mourning. Everyone was in shock, and businesses started to fall apart. People were not spending on unnecessary stuff, but only the essentials. From that day onwards, the business was very challenging. We had to cut costs and try to liquidate our existing stock. No more extra outsourcing for new merchandise; we had to close one shop just after a couple of months. We had to play it safe and sustain our income until things picked up again. I guess we Lebanese have big hopes and dreams for our country, regardless of all that has occurred.

Fast forward to 2006, again we hit the wall. Lebanon went into another war with our neighbouring country as we hit rock bottom. Everything was shut down for two months, and we were living in terror. I still had some flashbacks of when I was a child with my parents, but this time it was even more terrifying because, as an adult, you have more responsibility in having your own family. You become more aware of your surroundings.

Now, what is my next move? What Shall I do? I had a business to run, a family to support, and I needed to take care of the expenses, rent, employees, and merchandise. Lots of things to handle, and at the same time, you need to survive and generate income. You have kids to support, school to pay for, and rent due for the house. I will not bore you with the details; I think you've got the gist of things. These were hard choices that required my attention.

ASEAN Art was my prized possession, and I had been running it for four years now. Should I abandon my ship? Luckily, I spoke to my uncle, and he told me to join them in Saudi Arabia. They had a new business idea of a retail chain store selling and building materials, and they were looking for someone to run the business. I had experience in building material. What could possibly be the drawback? For four years and counting now, I have utter experience in the retail world. Great combination, right? Lucky me!

The funny thing was that I told myself; first, I would never go back and work in Saudi Arabia. Secondly, I would never again work with my uncle and his company with the same CEO. I accepted the offer, but this time, I wrote down my terms and conditions and took on the role of a Retail Manager. I didn't have much choice. I could look for a job like a typical person, but why the hassle! It was secure and fast. However, I made sure this time that I would not get fooled. Some people say that you live and learn from your previous mistakes, and that's exactly what I did.

The key lesson to learn here is that if you don't venture and take risks in what you want to do, you will never know the true meaning of success. Give yourself a chance and learn from your mistakes. This lesson has cost me lots of money and time, but it's a part of life. You fall, and you get back up again, and you never let yourself be defeated too quickly. You must accept and deal with every situation. A famous quote by Bruce Lee, one of my biggest idols 'Defeat is a state of mind. No one is ever defeated until defeat is accepted as a reality'.

New road, same thorns

I returned to Jeddah, Saudi Arabia, in September 2006. The environment in Saudi was almost the same, but I noticed some slight improvements in infrastructure and the living standards were of higher quality. The first thing I did was to look for a compound (we called them compounds because it is a living community space with all kinds of facilities such as swimming, sports area and is totally different from living in a normal apartment). I wanted to have a better life and eventually bring the family to come and live with me. My wife stayed behind in Beirut to watch over the business, and the plan was to close the company. Hana had a big burden and responsibility on her shoulders. She needed to manage the business and take care of three kids. What an amazing woman I have in my wife. I am so lucky to have her by my side. She is an incredibly supportive and understanding woman.

The company culture and team were familiar to me since I had worked with them before back in 1996. There were a couple of familiar faces, and it was quite important for me to settle in quickly and start being myself. I managed to adapt quickly to the working environment and start with a plan. But before that, I also needed to know my job responsibilities and connect with my direct team. I was the Retail Manager and in charge of five stores spread across Saudi Arabia. My objectives were to expand the business geographically, generate profitability, and meet revenue targets given by the higher management. I had a big role and was reporting to the acting General Manager for this business retail unit. I was supervising twenty employees across five stores. I constantly challenged myself to improve my team's efficiency. But how was I supposed to accomplish all that? Did I have the right skills and resources to do it? I told myself that I was there to learn and give a hundred percent. 'Gulf Depot,' the company I worked for, is a retail chain company selling building materials to construction companies and end-users (B2B and B2C) for their everyday use and requirements serving the construction industry.

Below was my initial action plan:

Step 1: Understand the current business model and learn how it operated to make sure that I had a balanced scorecard, i.e., customers, suppliers, employees' capabilities, qualifications, internal processes, and financial analysis.

Step 2: Put a map of Saudi Arabia on my office wall and have a vision and pinpoint the location of operation.

Step 3: Develop and expand our product portfolio to increase our basket size.

Step 4: Restructure the existing business model.

Step 5: Re-merchandize all shop layouts and create a brand image.

Once I had accomplished my above 'how-to' plan, I needed to find a way to implement it.

Step 1: Recruit and hire teams around me in different cities to accelerate this transition and scale up quickly yet efficiently.

Step 2: Locate prime locations for the shops by conducting a market survey and analysis. Make sure that the location will generate walk-in customers.

Step 3: Create a company policy and procedure manuals for all the employees.

I was travelling daily to different cities in Saudi. One morning I was in Damman and in the afternoon, I would be in Riyadh. It was a total nightmare and yet fascinating at the same time. I was young and full of energy. Plus, I was alone without my family around me. I guess that turned out to be a contributing factor for me to be able to work twenty-four seven, nonstop, and concentrate fully on my job with no distractions. As I have mentioned in a previous chapter, my family counts on me. That means working every day, with no time off. Occasionally I would manage to get a day at the beach. Time was of the essence, and I needed to prove to the management and myself that I could, in fact, do it.

From 2006-2009 I was the Retail Manager of Gulf Depot. I was always invited to the yearly board meeting with the group. These meetings were always entertaining, and I genuinely would have a good time. I was at least recognized by the higher management. One time, I had to do a presentation about my business unit, and it was the perfect opportunity to present myself as the guy that was there to make a difference. I guess in our organization; they were not fond of big titles, so I took that chance and announced my title as a General Manager in front of everyone. I was overconfident with my work achievement, and so I did not shy away. Basically, from that moment on, I became the

General Manager, which is ironic because I titled myself. I wasn't going to wait for my CEO to promote me knowing the history we had.

Saudi Arabia was booming in 2009. Money was flying everywhere, and construction sites were popping up like mushrooms. The government had to build a lot of infrastructures, roads, schools, housing, hospitals, and universities. The sky was the limit since the government had a big budget and surplus. I guess due to the crude oil boomed prices, barrel prices peaked at $165 back in 2008.

'Crude Oil Price – Macrotrends.net '

I took it as an opportunity to grow fast, and so I experimented. I sometimes opened shops for a couple of months, and if it did not work out, I would close and move it to another location. We had the luxury to do that due to our positive, strong cash flow. I really struggled in the beginning to manage their current employees. I was coaching and training the employees on how to deal with the customers and about product knowledge. I even created a training centre for recruitment. The objective was for them to go to our workshop to learn about the product and gain knowledge on how to apply it, and then pass the educational part before getting hired. We had a system and structure, which was created from my own determination and hard work. We had a brand image to preserve integrity, loyalty, and reliability. I was efficient, straight to the point, and would not take no for an answer. I have a slogan at work, 'there is no excuse' but also, 'if you don't have time, make time.' I needed fast, productive work, we were running against the clock, and I needed results.

I even learned how to delegate some tasks to those who reported to me. That by itself is an art on its own. You need to trust the team that surrounds you, as well as making sure their performance is to its best ability. I had a problem before in trusting people to perform the task at hand the way I wanted to. This was a learning curve for me. I learned about leadership and how to grow my company fast. I was micromanaging the operation, and over time I managed to understand how to delegate the tasks. Instead, I macro-managed and took a step back to look at the bigger picture as I surrounded myself with a good team. I trained them well and taught them to have the same mindset as me. It is not easy to find the right people and coach them, allowing them to follow you and be their role model. Please remember that as a leader, you have an objective to reach a particular target. One person can't reach that goal if he does not build and surround himself with a team that can be trusted and has excellent working skills.

What is my leadership style, one might ask? Basically, who am I? Well, I have come to find out that I have three main dominant styles of leadership.

1. Authoritative style: I like to motivate and inspire others to focus on end-goals. I set clear directions and standards. I do not accept failure; there is no room for error in a business environment that is challenging and competitive.

2.   Innovative style: I always encourage my team to come up with creative ideas and think outside the box. I want them to have inspiration in their work and sometimes define the rules.

3.   Pacesetting style: I am focused on goals and objectives, and with limited time, I show them how it is done and lead by example. I do more hands-on operations.

Taking charge and acceptance of its sheer responsibility is what the authoritative style of leadership is all about. A business environment should be high paced and competitive, which itself is a motivating aspect. The innovative style is to keep their minds sharp and their critical thinking, decision making and overall thought process agile and efficient. The pacesetting style is what the objective; the short term, intermediate and long term plans and strategies to see them through. Such a mindset was what led me to sufficient results. The following was the result of my work responsibilities as a G.M.:

1. I was reporting to the group CEO on a monthly basis.

2. I grew the business from five outlets to forty within a span of three years across Egypt, Syria, Lebanon, and Saudi Arabia: with a total of sixteen million dollars of profits.

3. I was managing a team of 140 employees with over forty retail showrooms and fifteen direct reports.

4. I have managed to increase the sales turnover by sixty percent over three years by opening new outlets and achieving profitable revenue in all branches.

5. I have managed to enhance the gross margin by four percent by negotiating with suppliers and getting yearly rebates.

6. I recruited and mentored new employees to increase customer satisfaction by fifty percent.

7. I directed and restructured supply chain processes by using a balanced scorecard to ensure a smooth running of the business by reducing the delivery time to customers down to twelve hours.

8. I introduced constant promotions, merchandising displays, along a hundred-page catalogue to create brand awareness and company image by also creating a company policy manual and procedure.

9. I developed an e-commerce platform to drive sales to a new Omni channel.

10. I established a loyalty program to boost customer footprint and retention rate by 20%.

One thing that I forgot to mention is that my family did not come and live with me in Saudi Arabia during these eleven years. I did not have a great work-life balance. I was alone, and I was commuting back and forth over the weekend to Beirut for two days. Of course, my family used to visit me during the school break, and the kids loved coming. Especially that there were so many activities to do, and I was friends with people who had kids. As I have mentioned, I was totally dedicated to my job. It took away from me being a father to my kids and missing out on this journey with them. It is a choice that I had to make to survive and provide for my family. Hana was very understanding, and we made that decision together. She was still running our business in Beirut for a few years, keeping herself busy for a while.

To compromise on the work-life balance, we decided to shut it down in 2010. During those years, I was making good money, so every year we used to spend summer vacations in different cities and countries with the whole family together. I even sent my kids to summer camp in Switzerland, Los Angeles, and New York. I wanted them to enjoy life the same way I did and the same way my parents allowed me. My wife and I used to travel on a yearly basis alone for two to three-day trips to London, Amsterdam, and other destinations, leaving the kids behind with their grandparents. We had great quality time, just the two of us, and we could afford to spend money. I did sacrifice being away from them but also provided them with a quality life.

Since 2016, Saudi Arabia started to transform. Society and lifestyle were somewhat normal. Entertainment, concerts, movies, women could drive and work. I had never been so happy with my life. Now things had totally changed. The one-hundred-and-eighty-degree transformation from the Saudi woman perceptive. Women could have more fun and could experience life outside of their homes. They joined the men in their working environment, and it was so lovely to see women working in the office. It brought joy and happiness, as the office space atmosphere was not filled with so much testosterone. It is good to have a balance. At the same time, Saudi Arabia had an economic crisis due to the crude oil prices crash that dropped to forty-three dollars per barrel. We had a slow downturn from 2016-2017. The business was very slow, and we were struggling. I had to adjust my business plan and take quick action to revive the operation and make it sustainable for a while. It was challenging, and I had to take care of and manage different stakeholders. I have seen the sky before, but I've hit rock bottom. Totally opposite directions, and a 180° turn in the ecosystem transformation. You learn new things and how to deal with it. Again, embrace every moment of it, no matter how good or bad the situation is. It is what will make you stronger as a person, a manager, and overall a better leader.

During the crisis, I told myself it was time for me to explore new career growth and opportunities to climb the ladder, considering there was no room to grow within my company. My overall dream was to become the CEO one day since I had the experience as well as the upper hand. I had a few discussions with my uncle during our regular lunch break, where I used to go to his house to get closer to him in hopes to get promoted by him. Every time I opened the subject for discussion, and he shut me down. Knowing that I had absolutely zero chance for career growth, and I was proposing some innovative ideas with no luck, I told myself why I should wait for a miracle? I needed to start thinking about setting my priorities in life.

I started applying left and right for a job and with no luck. Not a single phone call from a recruiter. To be honest, I was not quite comfortable leaving the business behind, especially one that I had built from scratch. But the ship was sinking, and the upper management did not want to invest and inject more money into it. I remember my cousin was studying for the GMAT exam and wanted to apply for an MBA in the top universities. You know me with my BBA experience; no way in hell I could do the GMAT and apply for an MBA. I always thought that it would be challenging for me and that I have been away from academic study for more than twenty years. I thought I was not qualified at all. I thought of it constantly and told myself that the business is ideal, and I would have more free time to study; it's my only chance to put the degree on my CV to be at least visible and add an extra value.

So why not invest time in education and self-development at such an ideal time? I would still be working in my current job and, at the same time, benefit from higher education, hoping it would lead me into a career shift or getting a C-suite position at a different company. On a side note, my eldest son Ryan was also going to university and studying electronic computer engineering. I guess I wanted to be a role model for my kids and show them that it is never too late to do your MBA, even at the age of forty-four.

Let me share with you a brief story about how and why I applied for the MBA program. After a long summer vacation in Miami with my Family back in 2017, I was sitting on my laptop and was browsing online. Suddenly a pop-up notification came up, and it was an ad for an MBA at Hult University. I was intrigued, so I went onto their website and applied online. Around ten minutes later, I received a call from the administration official who spoke to me and told me that I was accepted and welcomed me to the program. I was shocked and amazed at how easy it was. I called Hana immediately and told her the story. She told me that if I wanted to do an MBA, I'd better apply for the top five-ranked universities worldwide. She started to do her research and eventually came to a conclusion to apply for London Business School. The good thing about it was that there was no GMAT, and instead, there was something new called E.A. for Executive MBA. I found it interesting. Lucky me. Let me give it a shot, then I thought to myself, there's no harm in trying.

The lesson learned here is to trust yourself to succeed and never give up. Always think outside the box and explore new possibilities, yet also enjoy every moment of life. Learn to maintain a balance. There are always ups and downs. Be ready for plan B, no matter how small or ridiculous it may be. At least it is a plan. Some people don't even have an alternative or even a clue about what they are supposed to do in their life. They spend their entire life wandering and searching for their dream. You have the power to take control of your life, set goals, and objectives to achieve them. The future is waiting for you. A famous quote by Oprah Winfrey, 'The key to realizing a dream, is to focus not on success but its significance, then even the small steps and little victories along your path will take you on a greater meaning.'

The good thing is that I have no regrets in any decisions or choices I made in my life. I only embrace it.

Stage 1 of transformation

January 14th, 2018 was stage one of my transformation in life. I still remember it as if it were yesterday. We had our first class at the London Campus for a week. I flew from Beirut to London since I was in Beirut at that time with the family. I packed my bags with suits, and of course, some warmer clothes. London has different weather than I am used to. We had to establish our first impressions that the first day since you are, in a sense competing with other professionals just like you. It is always the first impression that counts. That's something worth remembering. Before I joined the program, I had done a lot of research and watched a couple of webinars about the LBS experience and how to extract value from it. The things that stuck with me the most was networking and career counselling. My mind was already pre-set in that direction and focused on those concepts.

On the first day of class, I met with my classmates, and most especially with my 'team' of four. These are the ones who would be with me for a year, working in groups for many assignments. We were glued together like kids going to school for the first time, with each one of us with a different background and nationality. Every day, we had lunch together and at night, dinner and drinks. I was so overwhelmed the first week, and I even struggled to cope with the professors' teaching, listening, and taking notes. Everyone had a fancy iPad and Surface Pros. I was the only one with the low-tech option of a notebook. I was outdated in this new era. I was among the eldest in the class; the average age of the class was thirty-six years old and a total of fifty-five classmates.

There was a lot of engagement during the class, and students were asking questions and interacting with the professor and amongst each other. I told myself: What the hell am I doing here? Did I make the right choice? Would I be able to survive this for two-years? Could I get a refund? Trust me, it's not a small amount. Compared to the other classmates, I would say that seventy percent were financed and sponsored by their employer. Therefore, they did not have much to lose. It wasn't their money.

For me, it was a big challenge, and I needed to keep my spirit up. If you think about it, when I was doing my undergraduate, I did not care much since I was not paying for it from my pocket, and I was not really focusing. Now my mind had totally transformed. First, I had matured so much, and second, I was a responsible grown man. I made that choice and was convinced by it; no one forced me to do it. It is crazy and intriguing how the human mind operates. Now, there wasn't any room for failure; otherwise, I would lose this whole tuition amount and not even earn a degree. To cut things short, my first week of MBA in London, I was super busy twenty-four-seven. I did not even have time to check up on my wife and update her over the phone on WhatsApp. It is like she did not exist at all. Going to my last day of the first week, the university organized a dinner party for us to enjoy, mingle, and let off some steam. One thing about the party is that people called me a 'party crasher' (I will come back to it later at the end of my core year). I sometimes got invited to a wedding because of my energy and dancing skills that I picked up over the year of blowing off steam from heavy loads of work. Of course, give me a drink and great music, and I am on fire.

I left London, came back to Beirut, and then flew over to Saudi for work. I spent one night with Hana, and vividly remember that I told her I was leaving the program. I didn't want to continue. I could not sleep at night due to my anxiety and stress during that week. I was super scared to fail. My mind was playing tricks on me, and the way I function, I needed to be systematic and have a structure and plan for everything ahead of me. For me, this MBA had a lot of variables and unknown elements. I don't know how to handle things if I can't see it or visualize it in my mind. How could I continue and survive? How are other people doing it?

Hana told me six simple words: 'Shut up Bitch and do it.' I love my wife, and she is my mentor. I told myself to give it another shot. My next class was in a month. The classes took place once every month for five days. This way, the work environments weren't really affected. On top of that, in between classes, you had a lot of assignments. Reading articles, books, case studies, exams, finals, and much more. I was studying daily for two to three hours nonstop. I even remember how I had ditched my friends for a while. I knew not contacting them is rude, but I was so focused that I just couldn't let it go. No joke. It was my luck that work was slow, and it's one of the reasons that I was able to do my MBA. I needed to leverage this ideal time and turn it to my advantage.

One thing I forget to mention. Apparently, the schools have something called an academic, social, and career representative. A volunteering role in coordinating between the program office and the professor. It is like an intermediate person that represents the class in terms of academia and also organizes social events during the week. The way the process works is that you volunteer yourself, and then you pitch it to the class so they may vote for you. There was no way in hell I was going to do that. I didn't want more attention or pressure. I had enough things on my plate already. Apparently, a few of my 'friends' had elected me and told me to pursue it. They needed me to be the academic rep. I don't know what they saw in me, and what was my qualification? I was shy in class and didn't even raise my hand much, but they saw me. I was helping them with their assignments during the first week before I knew it. I always liked to help others, and that is one of my core characteristics so that I can also learn from them.

I accepted this challenge and told myself if those friends believe in me, why not give it a shot and volunteer and pitch for the class? They even helped me with my campaign by promoting me left, right, and centre. I prepared my pitch for our next meeting in February. I rehearsed it daily to make sure it sounded good and professional. I was competing against two other candidates.

During the February election and pitching, I won with flying colours! Soon I became the most popular "kid" in school. Charismatic, plus I already had all the attention from my last night in London. Although my presentation was not as professional as the others, the audience trusted me. I wouldn't have voted for myself, but the eye sees what it wants to. From that day forward, I was the academic rep for a class of fifty-five students. I needed to represent their interest and the interest of the school. It was overwhelming for me, but I did enjoy it. I was their advisor, mentor, and teacher.

They called me twenty-four seven. Ihab, can you help me? Ihab, when is the deadline? Ihab I failed this class, what should I do? I needed to have all the answers, and I didn't even know how to help all of them. I was new in this experience as well, and I had to ask to the program officer different questions. I was the centre of attention. Even during the weekdays, I was the first one in class, and I needed to make sure that everyone was on time. I was the last one to go to bed at night. I needed to, though, didn't want to be an 'asshole' to my friends. I hated it. But I had a responsibility, and I took it seriously.

I was still having doubts about quitting the program. I couldn't handle the pressure of my studies, plus my peers' pressure. Again, I told Hana that I was quitting, and she again she shut me down. It took me like three or four months to really adjust to this studying environment. I was evolving months at a time and studying nonstop. I even created a study group in Jeddah, where I lived. We used to study during the weekend before the exam day. Everyone was asking me for help, but I was not a genius. I didn't have all the answers. I was only studying more than others and putting in more time. I remember during the exam, I was the first one out of the class. It was like a challenge/competition for me to finish first for reasons I won't reveal. It does not mean I did great, but I was confident that I would pass it.

During the program, we had a career coach, and I took this opportunity to have a one on one coaching session with Ki. We met every month. He was an amazing person and very understanding. He helped me a lot in setting my priorities straight, how to be visible on LinkedIn, how to fix my CV, and how to conduct interviews. We built a strong relationship. He used to give me a couple of tasks to do and a few challenges that I always managed to get done. He gave me feedback, advice, and tips. His famous quote was, 'you are planting seeds.' I started slowly and built my profile and brand identity. Trust me, it is not an easy task, along with a full-time job, on top of the burden I had from the courses. I will come back to Ki in the next chapter and how he played a key role in my journey.

From month to month, it was all too familiar; everything was the same – from 9:00 a.m. until 8:00 p.m., nonstop classes for five continuous days. After 8:00 p.m., partying and drinking all night. I used to go to bed at 1:00 a.m. daily for five days and wake up at 7:30 am sharp and was on campus by 8:30 am. It's like I was a robot. If you've seen the movie *Groundhog Day*, it was basically that for five days out of the month. I don't know how my body could keep going at my age. I was like a kid. You need to blow off some steam; otherwise, you would not be able to continue for long. I was a bad influence on my classmates. I would tell them to come and join us for drinks. I was dragging people to pubs instead of hitting the books and setting an example for them. I am human at the end of the day. I wanted to enjoy myself. I think it is a coping mechanism for me to release my stress and anxiety built up during the whole week. I was hiding it so well that no one even noticed. I kept my feelings and emotions to myself and never showed them to other people.

I took flights on the weekends to see my family in Beirut and then flew back to campus in Dubai. My kids had already given me a fun little nickname, "Nerdy." One thing about me is that I am very close to my children and wanted to be their friend also. My son was eighteen at that point, and even now, we still occasionally share a drink or two. I spent eight to nine months, commuting back and forth between Dubai and Beirut. The last day of the first year was in November, and the social rep organized a farewell party.

It was beautiful, and he managed quite the award ceremony. As you can guess, I won the award for "party animal." You might have thought I would have won "best president" or something like that, but no.

Part of the program is that you need to choose a GBA (Global Business Assignment.) You have the choice between six cities. (Beijing, Argentina, Mexico, Dubai, LA, Athens). I chose Buenos Aires because I had not been there, and it was a chance to explore a new culture and country. I decided to take my wife with me, and she was just as excited. At least it would be a gift from me to her for not being there during the MBA year, and to thank her for her continuous support. The trip was planned by the end of November. We decided to go for more than five days and explore the country. We had a fabulous time! Quiet and peaceful in the Patagonian mountain area. She stayed with me the whole time, and I was away during the day for a site class visit.

After 4:00 p.m., I was free. She got to know most of my friends and hit it off with them. We really did enjoy ourselves. The GBA was the best time ever for my MBA since there is not much pressure and studying to do. Plus, you meet different cohorts from other countries and programs. You get to mix it up and expand your network.

Once the core year came to an end, you still had the elective year, where you get to choose your own classes, dates, and program. This is where you specialize in one subject matter, depending on your priority in life. My next journey and elective would start from January of 2019, so I took a two-month break from studying.

My key lesson here, among other aspects, is to be visible, take risks, challenge yourself to extract boundaries, take advantage of every single opportunity in front of you, never say 'no' and forget the rest. You will do fine. A famous quote of Tyrion Lannister from *'Game of Thrones'*: 'Never forget what you are. The rest of the world will not. Wear it like armour, and it can never be used to hurt you.'

'AHA' moment

I started working on my CV and began applying for Jobs on LinkedIn during the MBA program as per Ki's advice. I even started posting on LinkedIn about retail insight in Saudi Arabia since it was my industry, and I needed to brand and position myself into my expertise on a bi-monthly basis. Trust me, it was not easy, especially at first, since I had the whole world's attention on me, and I didn't want to mess it up. Over time, I got used to it and enjoyed being on social media platforms. Every time we finished a class, I took a group picture and then wrote a summary post of what we have learned during that week. It is like key takeaways from the lesson in my perspective of specific topics. It's such a joy to have thirty likes and with over 3,000 people who view your post. Indeed the power of social media is illimitable. I remember one time for my graduation post, with my picture on it, and with a beautiful overall summary of my LBS journey, I got around 12,000 views with over one hundred likes. Of course, you add hashtags, and you tag other people on your post. It is a trick that you learn over time to accomplish. There are a lot of hidden things that only by practising will you master. It is an art.

My academic representative journey had been over since November of the previous year. What was next for me? I kind of liked all the attention I was getting, and it had grown on me. I needed to take on a new challenge and explore other opportunities. There was a club of London Business School called the Gulf Association for Alumni. This was the first time I had heard of such a club. I was intrigued and curious, so I joined that club on a WhatsApp group. They were having an election this year for a new president. I took that chance and applied for it. Of course, I was rejected because I did not have the experience, and there were other candidates before me waiting in the queue. On that WhatsApp group, I monitored every conversation carefully. I remember the new president who was in charge of the whole GCC Club posted that she was looking for someone to fill the Saudi Arabia Club in Jeddah, Riyadh, and Dammam cities. (The three major cities in Saudi Arabia). The LBS community in Saudi was huge, around 1,000 Alumni, and mostly based in Riyadh, the Capital. I immediately WhatsApped 'Evie' (the president) and told her that I wanted to meet her to discuss the opportunity. I decided to take a leap of faith and become the Jeddah Club leader for LBS Alumni. Another crazy challenge as I didn't know anything about organizing events and getting alumni to join the group. I was in Jeddah, and she was in Dubai. I told her the next time I'm in Dubai, in January, let's meet up to discuss.

I was planning everything in my head. I am an expert in planning and scheduling. I met and spoke to Evie for about five minutes, and she immediately said, 'yes, go ahead.' I was super excited about this new adventure and scared because, again, there was a lot of unknown down this path ahead of me. No club existed before for Alumni in Saudi Arabia except in Riyadh, meaning that no one heard of such a club before in Jeddah. I had to build this chapter from scratch and invite people to join. I didn't even know where to begin! I asked the school to send me the list of the Jeddah community database, and I would start from there. The list was a mess and could rather be termed as outdated. Only fifty percent responded, and that was only thirty or so people. I started hunting for people from left to right. I started texting, emailing, and posting on LinkedIn. I wanted to create awareness for this new group. With word of mouth, I managed to expand the group to about one hundred in the span of a month.

I had a fantastic start. I organized monthly social gatherings and quarterly keynote speaking events. Everyone loved me in the group, and I was getting the chance to network with people. The reason I was networking was to meet and connect with people for business opportunities. Why did I create this Club and put myself under more pressure? I think I only function under pressure, and I don't like being or feeling lazy. I like to multitask and love getting attention. I also created quarterly based newsletters and a WhatsApp group with email lists. I learned to get outside my comfort zone and shine away. I was a star! Every time I organized an event, I started posting on LinkedIn with a group picture and mentioned a few things about the events and hashtagged everyone in those pictures for more post-exposure and connections. I managed to increase my audience and traffic onto my profile. I was organizing and getting venues sponsored for free since we did not have a budget to pay for a venue. I became a master at pitching for free venues under the name and brand of LBS. I kind of enjoyed convincing people to give you something for free, and in return, to get their brand visible on LBS social media network.

I took seven elective courses in total during my MBA in both the London and Dubai campuses. My graduation ceremony was in July, and the whole family came along for seven days. We had an amazing time. I was so proud to be next to my kids and to introduce them to all my friends. I can't believe it has been more than 23 years when I took my graduation pictures. It just seemed like yesterday. We did exactly the same picture posture with my wife during my MBA graduation just for fun to compare it to the old pictures. Of course, now we also have our three kids next to us in the picture. It is such a nice emotional feeling to be surrounded by your kids for this moment. It is a memory that can't be forgotten. I was even awarded the Best Student Award from my peers, and there was a Gala dinner organized during the graduation ceremony held in July.

During the 2019 year, I was very visible and active on LinkedIn. I had managed to land ten interviews, all from big companies. Most of the interviews were through a recruiter who was job hunting and checking my profile. I guess I was so visible on LinkedIn and active with posting that it finally paid off. Before I conducted my interviews, I called Ki and asked him for feedback on how to prepare. He was amazing and helped me a lot, coaching me through everything quite well. None of the interviews worked out for me, unfortunately. One time, I had an interview with the

CEO of this company. Before I even sat down, he began to fire questions and issues towards me. It reminded me a lot of my interviews in Dubai. A few days later, I got a call from the company. They wanted me to join them, but I told them, "thank you, but no." I had learned how important the work culture was, and I was not going to sacrifice that. I did not want to be a part of such a culture; I knew better, I'd learned.

One thing that I hate in these interview processes is the whole waiting thing. From the moment you are selected, preparation, giving the interview, waiting for a 'yes' or a 'no.' You always keep your hopes up and excited, but then at the end, you become demotivated from possible rejection. I became so good at interviews that sometimes I was doing analysis for their business model when it was not even required. One thing I learned is to think outside the box and be different from the other candidates. I was lucky to have interviews with FMCG, F&B, Manufacturing, and Energy companies that I do not even have knowledge of, but I guess my profile seemed attractive to them.

I said to myself, "why not," and I was desperate for a new job before my MBA program was finished. I needed to land a job and start working immediately. I did not have the luxury to wait since I had responsibilities towards my family. The company I worked for started having financial problems, and the employee's salaries were delayed for a few months yet again. Does that remind you of something? Yes, I have been there before, and I knew how to handle this situation; I became an expert in handling hard cash flow issues.

On top of that, I needed to pay for my university tuition. So, it was an extra burden on my head. That made me push my limits and boundaries to react quickly and efficiently. There was no time to waste, and I was 'planting seeds' everywhere and anywhere during the entire year. I was a bulldozer moving forward nonstop without ever looking back. I was reaching out to my LBS Jeddah network and throwing myself out there, asking them for job leads. I was going from one event to another. I got very close to the British and the US Embassy because of my LBS tag brand. I was invited to attend their network events often. The sky was the limit for me. Nothing could stop me. I became very popular, and I really put in the time and effort to do all this because I needed to.

One day in June, before going to my graduation ceremony, I remembered that I had an old friend of mine who also happened to be my tennis partner. I am a big fan of tennis, as I mentioned before and never stopped playing during all those years. I became so good that I had become selective with the people I played. I did not want to waste my time, especially in sports, with someone who did not know the game. Call it arrogance, but I love tennis and enjoy it a lot but have no patience to waste with a 'non-pro.'

There is a saying 'Reach out to your dormant ties' from a famous LBS professor of mine. I had coffee with my friend, who was the owner and General Manager of a thirty-year-old company in Saudi Arabia selling building materials, and specifically all types of timber and wood related materials. I pitched him a crazy idea to have the same concept and setup that I had at the 'Gulf Depot' and transfer my knowledge and skills to his company, to open and operate retail shops, business development of new product range and training and branding this new division, amongst other ideas. A few days back, he called me and told me that he loved the idea. Now, I needed to prepare a business plan with feasibility research, which he would eventually check and offer me a job. Summer came, and my graduation ceremony was nearby. I was very busy with the family and travelling. I also had one of my last courses in September at the London Campus. At the same time, I was going back and forth, coordinating with his financial analyst for building the business plan.

I met the owner, 'aka,' my friend, in his Beirut office to discuss the final revised business plan back in August. Once the meeting was over, he offered me a salary package.

I was not very pleased by the offer since it was not a big improvement for me, plus my title would be Division Manager. Sort of a downgrade compared to my General Manager title. The purpose of doing the MBA was to climb up the ladder and to have a better career opportunity reaching the C-suite level. I did not know what came over me. Call it a spur of the moment or just utter craziness, I jumped and told him that I would do this job for him as a freelancer and not as an employee. Twofold: first, he was my friend, and I did not want to have a disagreement later. In case it does not work out, there would be no harm for both parties to adhere to agree and stop this project. Second, the offer was not intriguing, and I told him so. He loved this idea since it is very interesting for him not to invest much in me in a business sense. I told him that I would work out a couple of scenarios and then get back to him. It was a win-win situation for both of us, and I had, at least, secured something. Now I could breathe and relax a bit.

Armed with a bit of confidence, I went to London for my final elective, which was about negotiation and bargaining. A perfect course to finish in style, and I could use it in any business transaction or a pitch. I took my wife along with me during these two weeks of stay in London. Part vacation, part studying. I loved it when she came with me to London, and it was her second time being with me here for one of the courses. She hated coming to Dubai with me during these classes. September 2019 was the defining and turning point in my personal and professional life. I had a revelation I really cannot describe or put into words. But let me try:

I was having a one on one session with Ki, who is now my mentor, and was explaining to him my journey, my interview, the new project with my friend, and the freelance opportunity during this elective year. I told him that the offer and the job title were not great, plus I wanted to go out of this building material industry and try something else. He suddenly asked me: 'Ihab, why don't you start your own consultancy business?' That is when it hit me, and I had my 'Aha' moment. I don't know what came over me, but I instantly loved the idea but was scared. I told him Ki: 'I don't know anything about consultancy.' He said, do not worry. I will send you a couple of books for you to read. They will help guide you." I already had an existing client on my hand. What else did I need, right?

From that moment on, in my life, my thought process and mindset have totally transformed. I had someone to back me up and advise me. The whole week in London before my wife joined, I was reading, researching, writing a business plan, and building a road map. You know me; I need to have things clear in my mind and put forth a road and structure to follow behind. I had a plan in mind, and that was enough to start building on. The sky was the limit, and it was up to me to leverage my time to my advantage. I was free like a bird but also had more responsibility since you also need to secure more projects and clients adhering to the nature of a consultancy. You are not an employee anymore nor on a fixed payroll.

After my negotiation course was over, I had gained a couple of insights and knowledge on how to use it to my advantage. As mentioned earlier, my friend was waiting for a couple of scenarios for this freelance project idea. I used one of the lessons learned during the class and managed to secure the package deal I wanted. It was like magic. I'd even dropped an email to the professor and thanked him for this lesson. That means I had enough time to plan and search for new clients to cover the gap in finance, set up my business identity, logo, image, website, and company profile, amongst other things. Everything was perfect and planned out nicely in my mind. A dream come true!

Back to Jeddah in September, I submitted my resignation with my current company and went to Beirut to enjoy my time with family before starting this new venture in October. I was in Beirut working daily, reading, researching, writing content from my website, designing the logo, and building the brand identity. I used this idle time before I started the project to work on these issues. I came back to Jeddah before the first week of October to get myself ready for the new work culture and environment. The work part was a walk in the park since I was an expert and had already built this business model. I knew what to avoid and had learned from my mistakes.

Part of being a consultant was that I needed to be a good public speaker, conduct presentations in front of stakeholders, or even do some coaching. Back in Gulf Depot, I had conducted so many training and coaching sessions. Even during the MBA, I was a part of many presentations. Especially, being the rep, I had to speak out in front of an audience of fifty-five students. I always had butterflies in my stomach. I was not in control and confident in front of people. It was one thing to do presentations and speeches in front of your employees, but a completely different thing to do them in front of strangers and your peers.

As you know, I always liked to challenge myself and try new things. I remember during my MBA, one of my friend's advised me to join the Toastmaster Club. I did not really consider it much back then since we were already overwhelmed with a lot of education. I asked myself, why not? And to give it a shot since I have the time, and it would help during my keynote-speaking events at the LBS Club. I had searched for a couple of clubs in Jeddah and even visited a couple of them before deciding which one to join. I was shocked and surprised to see so many clubs and talent in Saudi Arabia from different backgrounds and nationalities. I told myself, if I could reach this level, I would have accomplished my objective and mastered public speaking for good. To be frank, one of my other objectives, to join public speaking is a twofold endeavour: to give a Ted-Ex talk one day, and second to become a professor and teach post-graduates. I am currently working on that particular objective.

I became an official Toastmaster member of the Odyssey Club in November of 2019. We met bi-monthly for regular meetings. I was in a hurry to make a speech at every meeting, but I needed to wait for my turn. There is a lot of work and preparation before giving a speech, you need to follow a topic of your specific pathway, and you need to complete all five levels. I was always rehearsing and recording my speech before going to the stage and writing my speech with an intro, body, and conclusion. It is really time-consuming. I was always practising on the weekends. After a few speeches, I started to excel at my public speaking and even won a couple of awards for the best speaker. Six months later, I also became an executive committee member of the Club without even pitching for this role, since the members loved me. Amongst other things, I started to write my diary, and this was recommended to me by an LBS friend in Jeddah. She is, in a way, my career advisor. I always like to surround myself with people I trust and who are professionals. I use my charm to befriend people, and I am very sociable.

There are so many lessons to learn here, but the key takeaways I would say are: think positive, always surround yourself with a mentor, never give up, be a good listener, and trust yourself always to move forward and succeed. A famous quote by Richard Branson, the founder of Virgin, goes something like this "If you ask any successful businessperson, they will always have had a great mentor at some point along the road''. You never know when your 'Aha' moment will hit you.

Stage 2 of transformation & pathway

'Life isn't about finding yourself. Life is about creating yourself.'
- George Bernard Shaw

2020 is stage two of my transformation in life, and I don't know what the future holds. I discovered my true potential and self and took a leap of faith. I am forty-six years of age now; I am halfway through my life in a way and became self-aware, which I will talk about in the next chapter.

To recap 2019, I was heading an LBS Alumni club with over a hundred members where we organize monthly social gatherings and also quarterly keynote speaking events. I joined the Odyssey Toastmaster Club, where we meet bimonthly and deliver a public speaking speech; I quit my old job, have a new project/consultancy job at hand with my friend. Last but not least, the company that I created, which I called 'Spectrum.' I guess that is more than enough to handle on one plate.

The beginning of 2020 was going great for me, but I was not promoting 'Spectrum' since I needed to prioritize the amount of work I gave to myself and to give a hundred percent effort for my project in order to have a good reference and reputation. I kept the marketing and promotion for Spectrum for a later stage, having the start date in July.

Anyway, So I was still networking and going to events and distributing my new business card to specific people but was not really in search of new clients. I needed to have a small team with me on a freelance term so that I can provide better services and be ready for it. I reached out to two of my friends who helped and were on board for a new adventure. I secured myself and locked them in. Being a consultant is not an easy task since you are liable for any advice and decision you recommend to a company. Your business plan and financial analysis need to be solid and bulletproof. There was no playing around since your name is on the line. That is why I assigned my whizz friend Karim in finance, who I trust blindly.

I was making side deals in between my jobs to secure extra income. One of my strengths is networking and connecting other people; hence I needed to monetize and use it to my advantage.

Now, let me dwell on the COVID-19 coronavirus days back in March. I am not going to bore you with the details, but I will tell you the opportunity that has aroused from this crisis. Some people lost their jobs, went into depression, some even committed suicide as per the news. Remember, I was stuck here in Jeddah, and there were no more flights connecting back that I may visit the family in Beirut on the weekends, which I did for the last thirteen years of my career. No hope in sight, no light at the end of the tunnel, panic, death, infection, garbage news on all the channels, articles about COVID-19 safety flying on all social media networks and WhatsApp groups, distractions, and nightmares everywhere. I mean, if you are not depressed, trust me, the news will make you feel anxious, give you stress, and even suicidal thoughts. Do I have corona or not? Am I asymptomatic or not? Well, first, you need to search google and understand this new 'jargon,' there is a whole vocabulary that we recently discovered. I am just trying to make a joke out of it because otherwise, you won't be able to live. I also guess one of my coping mechanisms happens to be humour. Let me add one more thing; I have selected memory, meaning that I just erase any information in my mind that I don't want to preserve during the night. It's like you are formatting your PC (also again, I don't know if people nowadays still practice this on their PC), so the next morning I start my day fresh and vivid. I just ignore and erase all the vibes that surround me and focus on key points.

I decided to think positively, clear my mind, and focus on my priorities. I even made a reflection journey of my life's timeline like a vision plan to see the "what" and if I did something wrong, to learn from it. Let me tell you what I did:

Step 1: Put a schedule and plan two weeks ahead of time.

Step 2: Laid down my personal financial report: Asset vs Liabilities to see where I stand and make sure that I am ready for this crisis.

Step 3: Manage my cash flow and expenses.

Step 4: Work on a plan and stick to it.

Step 5: Update it as I go along.

Step 6: Revisit and evaluate my original plan.

Well, I guess it is easier said than done. What is my plan, and how does one plan for the 'unknown'? The way I see it is that each individual can define his own plans and priorities. The most important thing is to have a plan so that you can work on it and have guidelines set ahead of your current time. Without a plan like we learn in life and in business school, everything will crumble down if you don't have a vision or a direction to where it is you are heading.

My action plan:

1. Workout.

2. Take online courses to elevate my skills and keep increasing my knowledge.

3. Watch educational webinars on your topics of interest. Hear experts and collect insights.

4. Have online meetings with your team.

5. Read books you like.

6. Learn new skills; for me, is cooking.

7. Most important is to have time to relax and enjoy your life. At night switch off and digitally detox. Such as watching Netflix, playing online games, PlayStation, or other things with your friends. It is important to maintain work-balance.

It is not enough to have a plan; now you need to make a daily schedule and spread it over two weeks. Keep your calendar always updated with upcoming events and set reminders on a to-do list. This by itself is a masterpiece and a full-time job to keep your mind preoccupied. It is an important time management skill.

Let's get into it. I think the subject of time management is more important than it seems. One needs time to achieve what one wishes to have in life. The more time you give into working for that you aspire, the more time you will have to enjoy those aspirations. The ones that say time cannot be bought are wrong. Putting in more effort than others and managing time right now can determine how much time you save for the future. The more you manage and plan your time, the less regretful you will be later. Matters in our life have a different level of importance that varies. A man who has everything under control, or the more commonly used "the man with the plan," has a certain aura of confidence. Which is a fact considering he has thought about what the future holds for him. Though many people lack vision, vision alone is not enough. Manifesting the goal into reality is; one cannot achieve it if he does not plan it. Be a step ahead by always being prepared.

Sit back, take out some time for this particular task, and write it down. Writing things down helps clarify your goals, priorities, and intentions. Write down the main goal, then write down all the actions you need to take that will lead up to it. So you write down what it is you want, whether materialistic or not. You then write down how exactly you get there. Is your current process taking you to where you want to be in life? If not, what should that process look like? Write it down. You now know your priorities. You can list them accordingly. Writing it down will help you when you find yourself in a situation where you need to choose which task to deal with first.

Based on what and how you prioritize, schedule your time for all the tasks accordingly. Note all the time that was being wasted, and add them to the tasks that demand more time. A keen benefit is that it becomes harder to get distracted and lose focus when you set a time limit to whatever it is that you're doing.

Do not forget to plan scheduled breaks for yourself in between your day. Whatever gets you going. Not taking breaks in between a particular job can impact the quality of your work, which is not something we are setting out to do. Jumping from one task to another is a recipe for disaster. Working smart is better than working hard. Never forget that.

You could be in any position in the hierarchy of life yet still be involved in tasks that need to be performed, varying from day-to-day. Tomorrow at work, you need to follow up with Brenda about her leaves, talk to your boss about the accounting software updates, and check the quality standard of a particular work. Anyone can remember these three things, I'd imagine if they really wanted to, but what if you needed to remember different stuff every day? Isn't that true for almost all of us? In general, human error exists, and we are bound to make mistakes that impact the quality of the outcome of a task performed. Again, writing it down, your responsibilities, what you need to do, and when you need to do it, plays an important role here. A to-do list is what I use as it helps me track all my previous tasks, track when I performed them, and to follow up on something that might have been missed. A calendar, alarm clock, notepad, the option are numerous; the participators are not. Stand out by doing what others are not. Only then can you take over what others are taking just a part of.

Mark Twain once said, "If it's your job to eat a frog, it's best to do it first thing in the morning. And if it's your job to eat two frogs, it's best to eat the biggest one first."

Now obviously, Mark did not expect us to eat frogs but instead expected us to handle matters with most concern first. When you set your priorities, the most important ones should be taken care of earlier in the day. Hence, being able to take care of it to our utmost potential. We start our day of getting up fresh in the morning, and as the day goes by, we get tired. Your daily tasks should be prioritized accordingly. Saving the least demanding for the last. This way, you can maximize accuracy on all tasks involved.

John Rampton, a former contributor at Forbes, refers to the famous 80-20 rule known as "The Pareto Principle," suggesting that 80% of results come from 20% of the effort put in. This is commonly used in sales, as 80% of sales typically come from 20% of the customers.

I found brilliance in his comparison to this principle to time management, saying, "When it comes to how you should manage your time, this principle can also be applied. 80% of your results come from 20% of your actions."

Strategic planning is required here. Make sure your to-do list is not pilling up, and try to put down the least amount of tasks you possibly can. You'd be surprised at how much work will get done if you focus on just the primary aspects. It could feel unnatural at first, but over time, this will condition you to scale up your efforts on the most important tasks."

Perfection is never avoided. Occasionally, it should. Especially when we talk about managing time, trust in your ability, verify all the input of the task and move on. Perfecting something we are working on is a never-ending process. Nothing can ever seem too perfect. What you might think is perfect might not seem that way to others. Have confidence and perform your task once, making sure that you finish the job in the time you have allotted yourself.

Charles Duhigg, author of the infamous "The Power of Habit," wrote about the term "keystone habits," which he defined as the habits that can transform your life, such as exercising, tracking what you eat, developing daily routines, and meditating. Many would say we are what we eat. I agree with a broader sense of the term, quoting Aristotle (father of Politics), and "We are what we repeatedly do. Excellence then is not an act, but a habit". We human beings are a creature of habit, and habits are a product of our thoughts which are influenced by our experiences and/or environment. Whatever tasks you choose to involve yourself with daily will be a big part of who you are as a person. So simply put, we do, as a matter of fact, choose who we are as well as we are the ones responsible for any changes required.

We spend our time in certain ways because we choose to. We do nothing without choosing. Although our choices are not always visible. We have the choice to do something or not. Each choice is based upon an anticipated reward. If you were not rewarded, you would not simply continue.

Learning to manage your time better will open up time to do important things. Rewards come from good time management habits.

Planning will keep you on track in achieving your goals and objectives. Abraham Lincoln reportedly once stated, "If I had sixty minutes to cut down a tree, I would spend forty minutes sharpening the axe and twenty minutes cutting it down."

Consider planning as "sharpening the axe." You have to take time out to create time. Planning is the difference between being REACTIVE and PROACTIVE. When you don't plan, you end up responding to the day's events as they occur.

What does a reactive day look like? You reach work in the morning with no clear idea about the day's activities. Things begin to gradually happen— with the whirlwind of activities, you respond to these various demands. You put a good amount of effort, but at the end of the day, you haven't accomplished anything significant. This approach is often referred to as FIREFIGHTING. If you don't determine what it is you want to achieve, you will experience frequent changes in your plans. You will experience a decision dilemma—if you don't determine what you want to achieve, others will be perfectly happy to fill your time for you.

You should have a full schedule and a lot on your plate to handle. I personally went the extra mile and used this free non-excuse time to connect with people on zoom meetings. I had nonstop zoom calls with colleagues, friends, and acquaintances. I saw an endless possibility to really reach out to strangers on LinkedIn and connect with people whom I met on webinars. Everything was possible at a click of a button and in easy reach for me since I was in my comfort zone at my home office. You can make meetings twenty-four seven and even on weekends.

The online experience has changed and accelerated my path for my consultancy business and making networking hassle-free, which makes the process much easier. You can now speak with someone in the US, Europe, anywhere anytime. No need to be well dressed during the meetings, just be you. I remembered meeting a company back in March, providing AI solutions, and I told myself now is the new era for digital transformation. I signed an agreement with them to be their representative in the GCC and promote their business. I would have an extra service offering potential clients. It was a door opener for me to introduce myself with a vital solution in accordance with the new current market demands. That by itself kept me busy for about two to three months during COVID-19.

In the meantime, I was still in touch with Ki, my mentor, and told him about organizing a Webinar with panellists for the LBS community. I was so addicted to watching webinars daily that I got curious and desirous, and it drove me to do one for myself. Again, I like to put myself on the spot, experiment, and see what the outcome will be. Well I guess, I already have the basics of public speaking skills from toastmaster and also have the skills to organize events from my LBS Club; so, it is only a matter of being able to present yourself on zoom in front of two hundred people. Scary right?

I launched my first webinar back in April. The feedback was great. Eventually, someone reached out and told me to moderate another webinar for them. I, of course, told them that I would do it since I was enjoying the exposure, visibility, and experience.

In parallel, I was uploading video content on YouTube and writing posts on LinkedIn as usual. Since that first webinar, I have now done eight different ones. It was crazy, and I was becoming an expert in event planning, moderating, and connecting people together. I became an influencer on LinkedIn, and people were asking me to promote their business within my network. How cool is that?

I always tell my friends and peers that with every crisis, there is an opportunity to create value and make a change and impact. As Sun Tzu said in his book, the art of war, "In the midst of chaos, there is opportunity. "I was unstoppable again, going at it with my full energy, dedication, and passion. I landed an interview with LBS for an alumnus, filming a story during the Covid-19, and was invited as a guest speaker for a coaching session with Ki. I talked about my experience with the career centre and, more relatively, to my relationship with Ki. Some of the new classmates reached out to me for a one on one coaching session; apparently, I had inspired them. Whenever a friend was feeling down, they would call, and I would boost their energy. I was bringing positive vibes to people around me, and I was a true role model and inspiration to everyone. I remember one of the books I read called '*The Secrets*' by Rhonda Byrne, and I recommend that people should read it. It is all about transforming the negative energy by surrounding your mind with positivity. Some people would say this is 'bull shit' but trust me as I speak from experience. Basically, you put a board in front of you, and you stick on it the things you want to accomplish. It could be related to money or health, basically, anything you want. The fact that you put it there, you are already transmitting positive vibes and energy. Trust me; you will accomplish your goals. One of my main goals back at age forty was to 'buy myself' or transform my body. I needed to lose weight and get a six-pack. It was a challenge, but I have managed to lose twenty kilos and have a nice shaped muscular body within three months. I don't know why I deviate from this subject, but anyhow it was worth sharing to emphasize the power of your mind how it can influence you. How you control, it is up to you!!! The psychology of the mind is a subject by itself, and I am no expert, but I have been through a few phases in my life of depression, so I can relate to it. No one is perfect, and everyone has issues, problems, and challenges. It is up to our wellness to combat each and every single one and overcome them. We are in control of our self and our mind.

August 4th, 2020, is one of the most tragic and biggest incidents in the history of Lebanon. It was ranked as one of the top three most powerful explosions after Hiroshima. We had a massive explosion at the port of Beirut, where more than 200 people died, and around 6,000 were heavily wounded and injured. There were more than three hundred thousand families without a home or a shelter. My wife and kids were in the house during the explosion, and thanks to God, they were luckily not injured; I was still in Jeddah locked up due to COVID-19 and flight restrictions. Hana, I, and all the Lebanese people were under a heavy shock for a couple of weeks.

We told ourselves; it is time for us to move out of Beirut and start a new life. Our two sons got accepted to study engineering at McGill University in Montreal, Canada, and will start classes in September for the fall. The next step will be for my wife and daughter to come and live with me in Saudi Arabia.

On top of that, I have decided to complement my consultancy business. While writing this book, I have decided to become a certified coach since it has become quite a new trend, and I can offer coaching sessions to my clients while advising them at the same time. It is like a win-win situation, and it can also help me achieve my dream of becoming a professor one day and teaching students at a university. I always had this need to coach deep inside of me, and now it was time to give back to the community with my knowledge, experience, and to monetize it. Now, I am armed with knowledge, wisdom, and experience. I have decided to write this book and share it with the world.

I believe new projects and ventures will always come across my path. A new idea was evoked with me to start my own Podcast series 'Pathways to Business Success,' which is also ironically my book title. No one truly knows what the future holds before them. It is all on us to shape our destiny and faith to create our path and trace our life's journey.

Key takeaway lessons: Simply take a leap of faith in yourself. Nothing of value is accomplished without first believing in yourself to take the jump. Martin Luther King once said, "Faith is taking the first step, even when you don't see the whole staircase."

Chapter 3: Know yourself

'The emotional brain responds to an event more quickly than the thinking brain. People tend to become more emotionally intelligent as they age and mature.'

Daniel Goleman

Before a candidate joins the MBA program, we all had to complete a 360-degree self-evaluation assessment test. It was interesting and intriguing since it was the first time I had ever heard of such a test. After that, you were assigned to a coach that would analyse your results and help you work on some areas of improvement. You would have a one on one coaching session, and she/he would try to understand you personally and give their recommendation.

My first session with my coach was a bit tense since it was like sitting down with a psychologist. You do not want to look like a fool or seem weak since you are in a business school and not at the doctor's office. Of course, all the information was kept confidential between both parties. The more input you give to the coach, the more beneficial it will be to you, and the more valuable it will be for your growth and learning. We are here to learn from the best, right? During our discussion, and according to my results (Diagram 1), I had a low depth of emotion; and I also needed to boost my self-confidence level and be more resilient as per (Diagram 2). My coach recommended I read a book about Emotional Intelligence to learn more and understand myself better.

EQ (Diagram 1)

Depth of Emotions				
Very Low	Low	Average	High	Very High

32

33   43   58   68

Emotions are unimportant, limited in range, controlled

Emotions are important, responsive, wide-ranging

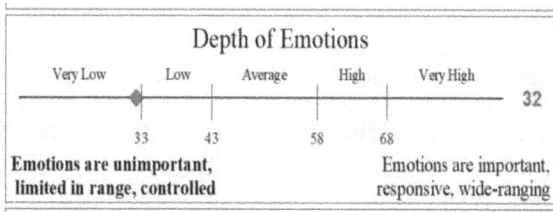

No Resilience (Diagram 2)

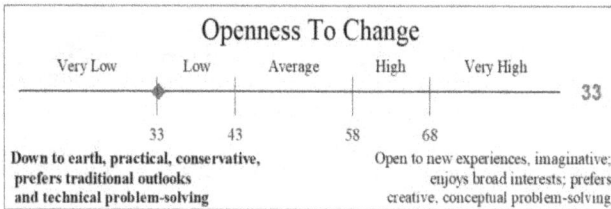

Openness To Change				
Very Low	Low	Average	High	Very High

33

33   43   58   68

Down to earth, practical, conservative, prefers traditional outlooks and technical problem-solving

Open to new experiences, imaginative; enjoys broad interests; prefers creative, conceptual problem-solving

Before I even read the book, I needed to google EQ since I was only aware of IQ. One additional note as per the coach's evaluation, and my 360 degree, is that I was an introvert. If you google introvert, you'll get exactly the response you're probably thinking of. "A shy, reticent person." As I have mentioned at the beginning of my book, I was an, in fact, an introvert. If you would like to know how to overcome being an introvert, I will try to give you the following steps and tips. Remember that these answers are only related to my own perspective and experience.

Step1: Be visible, get out there, and be heard.

Step 2: Increase your curiosity, do not be afraid to raise your hand and ask questions.

Step 3: Step outside of your comfort zone.

Step 4: Be yourself, reach out to people, and be a good pro-active listener.

Step 5: Explore and experiment.

I will try to give you examples for each of the following steps based on my personal journey so that I can put this context into perceptive for you:

Step 1: During my MBA, I applied for a volunteering role as an academic rep.

Step 2: I was always asking questions during the class, and I was trying to be visible.

Step 3: I built an LBS Alumni Club in Jeddah.

Step 4: I was reaching out to strangers and adding them to my group. I was not afraid to meet people and connect with them over the phone.

Step 5: I started organizing and moderating webinars besides the keynote speaker events.

If you follow the steps above, they will help lower the gap from being an introvert to becoming an extrovert. Since I shifted gears from an introvert to an extrovert, people have noticed the change and are now coming to me for advice and coaching.

Before I dive into this chapter, let me tell you that one of the most important aspects of a person's life is to know himself and discover his true identity. A person would be lost if he or she did not understand the meaning of life or have a sense of direction or motivation. You need to discover your potential, explore new ideas. Basically, ask yourself: "Who am I?" There is a world out there that it is trying to tell you who you are; there is a world in here that is trying to tell you who you are. The question is, where do you mark your X?

Some people spend years and still cannot find the answer. To tell you the truth, my assessment report, it was telling me that I did not know myself. I was not self-aware and did not have the priority to grow and develop my true self. My score was low, and the way they explained it is as follows:

'People are likely to see you as someone who lacks self-insight. They may as well see you as someone who is highly talented but will likely also see you as someone who does not really understand their own weaknesses and someone who may not be able to step back when others would be best suited for a particular role or situation'.

The other weak point was not being resilient. I do not like changes, and I have a tough time adapting to it. Something interesting is that I am programmed like a robot. I am a bit stubborn and cannot deviate from my course of action. My score was low, and the way they explained it, as reflected in the following results:

'People are likely to see you as someone who tends to be narrowly focused and not open to change. Low scorers are likely to be unable or unwilling to deal with the conflict that change creates and not be sufficiently persistent in pushing for change as roadblocks emerge.'

From that point onward, I knew I had areas to improve upon.

- For openness to change, I needed to increase my intellectual curiosity and be more resilient.
- For the knowledge and development of myself, I needed to be more self-aware and demonstrate strength to others.

Easier said than done. How can you overcome and improve them, one can ask? As per my coach's recommendation, I researched about EQ, watched a couple of YouTube videos, read articles, and did an EQ test on "Mindtools" website. Basically, I was working on my weak spots in order to try to analyse and understand them better and try to work on them. I found out that the father of emotional intelligence is Daniel Goleman, who wrote a book titled 'Working with Emotional Intelligence. 'I highly recommend that you read this book. I am basing this chapter on his findings and inspiration. I'll try to give you a short summary to the best of my abilities.

Growing up, I wouldn't say I had what is commonly known as a hard life. If I were to list a con of such a lifestyle, it would be that when you get out there into the real world, a place where you need to meet, deal with, manage and convince the not so privileged people, there will be a contrast between your communicational skills and overall mentality vs them who had to strive to survive at an earlier age, or perhaps their parents had to go through a certain struggle while reflecting their dilemma's on to their children, thus creating a certain situational awareness.

I felt this contrast the most in the first few days at my first sales job. That's the thing about a sales job though, it can teach you a lot about communication, and how to get a deal closed, how to target the clients need and play around it, create the need of your product/service and so on. How to say, when to say and what to say, skill a sales personnel knows all too well.

It is through the nature of my job, and the contrast of working in different countries while managing major responsibilities is what built a higher emotional intelligence within me. To deal with obstacles, to look at tomorrow as a whole new day, to avoid negative thoughts, recognize what you feel and focus on the positive, as well as a strong determination and self-belief to deliver what is expected of me. This came to me with time, with practise through the years of my occupation along with the nature of what I was doing.

Understanding Emotional Intelligence:

Over the last two decades, roles have become more customer orientated and knowledge-based, with the need to work together as a team. Management is all about getting work done through other people, some of whom you have no direct authority over. Goleman defines emotional intelligence as: *"Understanding one's own feelings, empathy for the feelings of others, and the regulation of emotion in a way that enhances living"*. EQ may be more important for personal success than IQ, and unlike IQ, the EQ can improve.

Goleman describes EQ in terms of five domains that are split into four quadrants, as listed below:

<u>Five Domain</u>s:

1. Knowing your emotions.
2. Managing your own emotions.
3. Motivating yourself.
4. Recognizing and understanding other people's emotions.
5. Managing relationships (i.e., managing the emotions of others.)

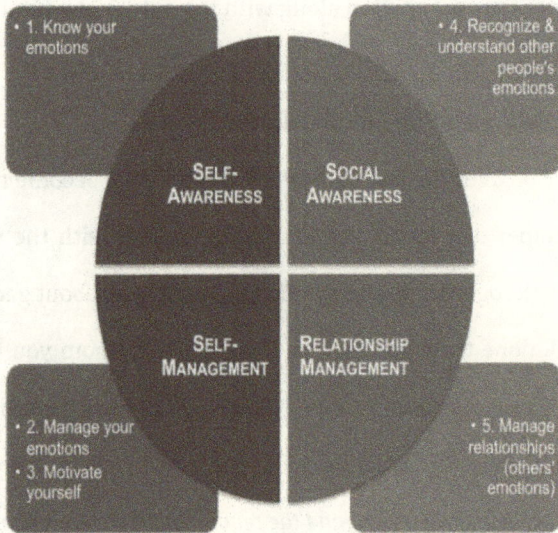

Two of the domains are related to personal competence, and two are related to social competence.

Personal Competence

Self-Awareness: This means that you need to understand how you feel and be able to accurately assess your own state of emotions. This includes *self-assessment*, i.e., understanding your own strengths and weakness, and *self-confidence*, i.e., the ability to ground oneself so that you are secure and self-assured in whatever situation you find yourself in.

- Self-management: Aims to build the understanding that you gained with self-awareness and involves controlling your emotions so that they do not control you.

Social Competence

1. Social awareness – involves expanding your awareness to include the emotions of the people around you and including empathy and organizational awareness.

2. Relationship Management – Means using awareness of your own emotions and of others to build stronger relationships. It also incorporates your ability to communicate, persuade & lead others, and develop strong working relationships.

   Goleman's definition of emotional intelligence proposes four broad domains. These consist of 19 competencies as follows:

Self-Awareness

1. Emotional self-awareness.
2. Accurate self-assessment: Knowing your strength and limits.
3. Self-confidence: a sound sense in one's self-worth and capabilities.

Self-Management

1. Emotional self-control.
2. Transparency: Honesty and integrity-trustworthiness.

3. Adaptability: Flexible to adapt to changing situations or obstacles.
4. Achievement: Improving performance to meet the inner standards of excellence.
5. Initiative: Ready to act and seize an opportunity.
6. Optimism: Seeing the upside in events.

Social Awareness

1. Empathy: Sensing others' emotions.
2. Organizational awareness: Reading the current decision network.
3. Service: Recognizing and meeting followers, clients, or customer's needs.
4. Inspirational leadership: Guiding and motivation with a compelling vision.
5. Influence: Wielding a range of tactics for persuasion.
6. Developing others: Bolstering others' liabilities through feedback and guidance.
7. Change catalyst: Initiating, managing and leading into a new direction.
8. Conflict management: Resolving disagreements.
9. Building bonds: Cultivating and maintaining a web of relationships.
10. Teamwork and collaboration: Cooperation and team building.

Can EQ be developed?

This is the most important part of this chapter.

Research has supported the idea that emotional intelligence

competencies can be significantly improved over time.

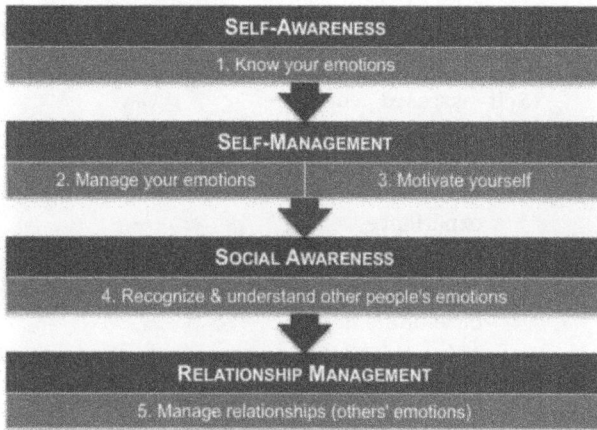

SELF-AWARENESS	
1. Know your emotions	

SELF-MANAGEMENT	
2. Manage your emotions	3. Motivate yourself

SOCIAL AWARENESS
4. Recognize & understand other people's emotions

RELATIONSHIP MANAGEMENT
5. Manage relationships (others' emotions)

Personal Competence

Personal competence consists of self-awareness, self-management, and self-motivation.

Self-awareness:

The ability to recognize your own emotions and their effect on yourself as well as other people. It is the foundation of EQ.

A person with a high level of emotional self-awareness will:

- Know which emotions he/she is feeling.
- Realize the links between their feelings and what they think, do, and say.
- Recognize how their feelings affect their work performance.
- Have a guiding awareness of their values and goals.

- Adopt behaviours that minimize the effects of their own emotions in a given situation.

Self-assessed people are:

- Aware of their strengths and weaknesses.
- Reflective and capable of learning from experience.
- Open to candid feedback and new perspectives.
- Interested in continuous learning and self-development.
- Able to show a sense of humour and perspective about themselves.

Self-confident people are:

- Exude 'A strong sense of one's self-worth and capabilities'

- Demonstrate certainty about their own values and capabilities.
- Exhibit a strong presence.
- Show a high level of self-assurance.
- Display a willingness to express an unpopular opinion or stand up for something that is right if they truly believe in it.
- Ability to make quick decisions even in uncertain and pressurize circumstances.
- Believe that they can control the direction of their lives – and they do.

Self-Management:

Build your own-self-awareness using self-control and willpower to ensure your emotions do not control you, regardless of the situation. Use what you know to manage and motivate yourself.

Self-control

-   Managing impulsive feelings and distressing emotions.
-   Stay composed, positive, and unflappable even in trying moments.
-   Think clearly and stay focused under pressure.

Trustworthiness

-   Act ethically and above reproach.
-   Build trust through reliability and authenticity.
-   Admit mistakes and confront unethical actions in others.
-   Taking a stand for tough principles even if they may be unpopular.

Conscientiousness

-   Meet commitments and keep promises.
-   Hold themselves accountable for meeting their objectives.
-   Organized and careful in work.

Adaptability

-   Smoothly handle multiple demands, shifting priorities, and rapid change.
-   Adapt their responses and tactics to fit fluid circumstances.
-   Versatility in viewing events.

Achievement orientation

-   Set themselves challenging goals.
-   Measure their own performance against those goals.
-   Actively seek out information to get the job done.
-   Use their time efficiently.

Innovativeness

- Seek out fresh ideas from a wide variety of sources.
- Entertain original solutions to problems.
- Generate new ideas.
- Have fresh perspectives and a risk-taking thought process.

Self-Motivation:
Striving to improve or meet a standard of excellence.

People with such competence:

Achievement drive:

- Results-oriented, with a high drive to meet their objectives and standards.
- Set challenging goals and take calculated risks.
- Pursue information to reduce uncertainty and find ways to do a better job.
- Learning how to improve their performance.

Commitment:

- Readily make personal or group sacrifices to meet a larger organizational goal.
- Find a sense of purpose in a mission larger than themselves.
- Use the group's core values in making decisions and clarifying choices.
- Actively seek out opportunities to fulfil the group's mission.

Initiative

- Seek out fresh ideas from a wide variety of sources.
- Entertain and create original solutions to problems.

- Generate new ideas.
- Have fresh perspectives and take risks in their thought process.

Optimism

- Persist in seeking goals despite obstacles and setbacks.
- Operate from the hope of success rather than the fear of failure.
- See setbacks as due to manageable circumstances rather than an innate flaw.

Social Competence

Social competence is made up of social awareness and

relationship management

Social awareness

Empathy

- Actively listen to what others say.
- Show they understand and appreciate others' views on current issues.
- Focus on attaining the goal or task without much conflict.
- Understand where emotional boundaries start and end.

Organizational awareness

- Understand the rationale behind their organization and its structure.
- Know how to get things done within the organization.
- Understand both client and vendor organizations.
- Act with the client's best interest in mind.

Service orientation

- Ability to carefully question to identify issues that are affecting an individual's performance.
- Identify or adapt situations so that they provide an opportunity to improve their productivity and satisfaction.

Relationship management

Succeeding in the competency of relationship management is directly related to your success in social awareness and your level of personal competency. This is because management is all about getting work done through other people, some of whom you have no direct authority over.

Influence

- Build consensus through persuasion and clear presentation of cases.
- Offer and gain support from others.
- Are trustworthy.

Leadership

- Lead by example.
- Inspire others to achieve a goal or view a particular vision.
- Truly delegate tasks and accountability.

Developing others

- Recognize and reward accomplishment and strong traits of individuals.
- Regularly challenge and offer new opportunities to the team.

- Provide constructive feedback to facilitate efficient development.

Communication
- Effortlessly adapt to the emotional context of the exchange.
- Focus on attaining objective by acknowledging others' views.
- Listen carefully, seek mutual understanding, and welcome the utter exchange of information.
- Foster open communication and stay receptive to bad news as well as good.

Change catalyst
- Do not hesitate to challenge the way things have always been done.
- Recognize barriers to change and seek resolutions to get rid of them.
- Act as a catalyst for change.

Conflict management
- Meet potential or existing conflict from the point of knowledge and strength.
- Have the ability to read underlying emotions within groups.
- Be open-minded and willing to embrace different perspectives.

Building bonds
- Be widely respected and appreciated.
- Cultivate a broad personal network that incorporates colleagues, professionals, contact, and friends.
- Keep them involved, informed.

Teamwork and collaboration

- Ensure the objective is defined and understood by all.
- Behave in a way that others adopt on their own.
- Demonstrate that they value all contributions.

Key points:

I have tried to put EQ in a nice framework so that you can adapt to it and start building your own self-awareness and leverage the defining point in your life. The rest will be up to you to whether to walk down this path or not. No one can make you listen, but you. Whether you believe in it or not is up to you. Some minds only see what's tangible in front of them. You need to freely open your mind to a whole new dimension and explore its versatility. Consider it a dream, and you have nothing to lose. Work on some of your weak links to improve them. Discover yourself through others. If you do not know your true self, then you can't read and walk towards the next chapter. Start today, and believe me, you will not regret it. Research EQ. Read articles, and more especially Daniel Goleman's book, or even watch some of his short videos on YouTube if you don't have the time to read. I can only impart the words of wisdom I have to inspire you to reach your ultimate potential.

'If you can't fly, then run. If you can't run, then walk. If you can't walk, then crawl, by all means, keep moving' Dr Martin Luther King Jr.

Chapter 4: Brand identity – Stand out from the crowd

'Simplicity is the essence of universality.'

Mahatma Gandhi

Once you've improved your self-awareness and feel comfortable in your own skin, it is time to build your profile and your personal brand. You need to start working on yourself because this is the part of your transformation journey where you become your own entrepreneur. Once you feel it, then you can start experimenting and moving forward toward success. The opportunities of the modern era are limitless. Seek anything and everything, be curious and open to knowledge. It is only a matter of time that you find something worth pursuing until the end.

I remember one day, I wanted to test the hypothesis of my own self-awareness. I conducted a standout assessment to measure my role and strength. I found out that this assessment was quite sharp and really boosted my self-confidence. The picture below shows the result of my role and strength. I was an advisor and a connector! You may want to know that this assessment will always evolve and change throughout your journey because it is only an indication of your current path and timeline. Needless to say, you have to put in the work if you want the results.

Advisor

Connector

Ihab Tabbara

What do you think when you hear the word "Advisor?" The mind draws up images of an office with a desk filled with paperwork. What can you do to not think of those things?

You begin by asking, "What is the best thing to do?"

Part of the thrill comes from finding out that all the answers are instilled in no one but you. People come to you. You don't want to be the one who makes the changes, but you get excited at the thought of people coming to you for insight and your better judgment. You love to be the expert, so you're constantly on the lookout for information that will help people make better decisions.

As you're paying more attention to the world around you, you begin to notice the "Devil in the details" that help you provide better advice. You know that each piece of advice has to be tailored to the unique characteristics of the person's situation. You can be demanding and opinionated, but "good enough" is never really good enough for you. There is always a better way, a better arrangement, a better solution, and you come alive when you are called upon to find it. When you do, you don't question your decision. The reason people seek your advice is because you are assured and confident in your intuition. You are instinctively aware and take great pride in it.

What is a "Connector?"
You begin by asking, "Whom or what can I connect?"

You see the world as a web of relationships, and you are excited by the prospect of connecting people within your web. Not because they will like each other, which they might, but rather because of what they could create together. Your mantra is "One plus one makes three." Or thirty. Or three hundred."

On your most optimistic days, you see no limit to what people with different strengths and perspectives can create together. You are naturally an inquisitive person. You're always asking questions about each person's background, experience, and skills. You know instinctively that each person brings something unique and distinct to the table. This is something, no matter how small, that might prove to be the vital ingredient. In your head, you store a large network of people with whom you've met, learned about, catalogued, and positioned somewhere within this network. Each person has a link to at least another person, each with an open port for another link to be added. People are drawn to you because you are so obviously passionate about their particular expertise and because you have so many practical ideas about how their expertise can be combined with others and manifested for a particular desire. You enliven and enlarge others' visions of who they are and what they can achieve. You display the potential in others, abilities that they themselves do not know they have. You are a connector, weaving people together into the fabric of something much larger and more significant than themselves. You help them paint what they do not know is the bigger picture. You help them connect the dots from their individuality to their desires and show them how their potential leads the way. It is hard for us to reach a potential goal if we lack connection. Not impossible, but near to it. Manifestation requires you to leverage the ones around you. Talk to people, and much like any other habit, you will build it too. Look at my story; that's exactly what I did. Practice makes perfect.

So when I read the report, I told myself, "'Oh my God.' That's so me!!!" Accordingly, what I did was to use this tool and work around it and try to position myself and my own identity. Of course, you pick the one that is most suited to you since you know yourself the best.

Building your personal brand

The good news is that you already have a personal brand, whether you know it or not. In fact, you are a brand. You may or may not be aware of your brand identity, and if not, that's okay. That's what I would like to help you uncover. Your own personal brand!

What do we mean by personal brand? What is it exactly? A personal brand is everything that you bring to the table. Because what you have to offer, no one else can. It includes your skills and your values, as well as how you add value to any situation. We all have different experiences, which leads to a different thought process, and so different ways we interpret matters of the universe. Because of this universal process, each and every single person's individuality is unique to themselves. Think of a business contact you know of. What first comes to mind when you hear their name? Now think about yourself for a moment. What do you think comes to the mind of others when your name pops up in conversation? Marketers McNally and Speak define personal brand stating: *"Your brand is a perception or emotion, maintained by somebody other than you, that describes the total experience of having a relationship with you.*

Ironically, your personal brand is ultimately not about you – it's the perception others have of you based on the value you provide them. You can only build value when you possess it, and you cannot own value if you are not curious-minded. If you are not open to any or all sources and perspectives of knowledge, you will suffer. We don't want that, do we?

You should ask yourself a couple of questions based on the graph below to identify your value:

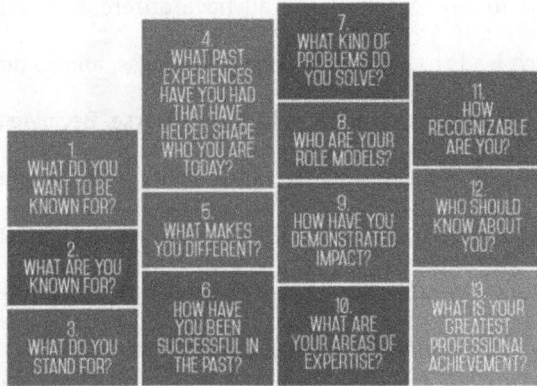

1. WHAT DO YOU WANT TO BE KNOWN FOR?	4. WHAT PAST EXPERIENCES HAVE YOU HAD THAT HAVE HELPED SHAPE WHO YOU ARE TODAY?	7. WHAT KIND OF PROBLEMS DO YOU SOLVE?	11. HOW RECOGNIZABLE ARE YOU?
		8. WHO ARE YOUR ROLE MODELS?	
2. WHAT ARE YOU KNOWN FOR?	5. WHAT MAKES YOU DIFFERENT?	9. HOW HAVE YOU DEMONSTRATED IMPACT?	12. WHO SHOULD KNOW ABOUT YOU?
3. WHAT DO YOU STAND FOR?	6. HOW HAVE YOU BEEN SUCCESSFUL IN THE PAST?	10. WHAT ARE YOUR AREAS OF EXPERTISE?	13. WHAT IS YOUR GREATEST PROFESSIONAL ACHIEVEMENT?

Identify your values:

You probably know your company's core values all too well. Maybe you can even recite them. But what about your own values? You probably know them inherently, but have you ever truly articulated them? Identifying your values is foundational to exuding your brand. It is the core of who you are and what emanates to others.

Companies that stick to their core values are more recognizable and successful in the marketplace. The same holds true on an individual level. Not only are they more recognizable, but they are also more fulfilled. When work and life are aligned with your values, that's when you are at your best. You are positioned to succeed. When work and life are misaligned with your values, you experience unhappiness, unrest, and fatigue. You start to pick up bad habits and develop practices or behaviours that do not align with your personal brand and core principles. This is clearly not where you want to be. Sometimes, we end up here because our values have changed over time. This is normal. When you are starting your career, for example, you may highly value money, success, and doing whatever it takes to propel yourself forward.

As you age, you may highly prioritize balancing work with time for friends and family. The point is, your values evolve over time, and what you value in work and how you need to be positioned for success changes over time, too. Most of us have vague notions of what we value, but if prompted, we may not be able to articulate what is truly important to us. Sure, we know the things that societally we know we should—and likely do value. Things like family, friendship, and utter peace. But what matters to us as individuals that make us our unique selves?

What Do You Value?

EMPATHY
COMPASSION
UNITY
Balance
BEING THE BEST
COMMITMENT
LEADERSHIP
OPENNESS
INTELLIGENCE
UNDERSTANDING
CURIOSITY
Dependability

INQUISITIVENESS
SELFLESSNESS
Equality
ACCOUNTABILITY
USEFULNESS
Determination
POSITIVITY
AMBITION
Spontaneity
FAIRNESS
Generosity

Once you have identified your value, you can now move on to the positioning part:

Positioning:

I believe positioning is a fundamental aspect of your personal brand. What separates the 99% from the 1% is not only talent, skill, expertise, or ability, but also these three positioning factors:

Power positioning:

Desire is a function of VALUE + SCARCITY. This is why commodities are cheap, but rare gems/metals are expensive. When the right person finds you, they should see YOU as the "one and only" solution to their problem. The goal is to MAXIMIZE demand and MINIMIZE supply so you can increase your positioning the way you see fit. Power positioning is where the battle is won or lost; no amount of 'marketing' is going to save you from poor positioning.

Result mechanism positioning:

This part is a bit tricky since your time is valuable and doesn't scale. What scales better than time? RESULTS and this is what you should be focusing on. HOW? By providing the 'mechanism' through which you will help a certain individual achieve results. You also need to differentiate that mechanism from anything else they see in the market, thereby commanding 'value' and having a different position.

Leadership positioning:

A person will only reach out to you if you have the HIGHEST degree of confidence in yourself. So how do you inspire confidence? By proving to the person that you are the best choice through leadership positioning. The number one factor that separates 'winners' from 'losers' is insights and information. He who is open, willing to teach his knowledge to others while ready to comprehend what is new to him, is a winner. He who understands that before changing the world, he needs to make his own bed first, he who focuses what he lacks in, he who has the will and determination to accomplish his dreams and willing to put in the work, he is a winner. He who values his work-life just as much as his he values his family is a winner. It all depends on you on how you want to be seen by the world. You want to be seen as a real leader and expert in your market so that an individual can solve his problem with a healthy amount of confidence and have a pipeline full of high-quality prospects or simply be a 'loser.' Now, let us move on to the Networking part which will complement the section above.

Networking:

Networking is an opportunity for your personal brand to shine. In-person networking events, however, can cause apprehension for even the most experienced of the executives. However, attending such events can have a huge impact on your career trajectory; therefore, it is vital that executives make time for networking in their schedules. It is important to start building your network as soon as possible. The key to efficient networking has always been to build a network before you actually need one. It is essential to remember that networking should always be a mutually beneficial practice; you should try to have something to offer those with whom you seek to connect. While online networking has dramatically increased in relevance with the rise of social networks and can help with making connections quickly, in-person networking helps to develop deeper relationships. To assist you in your goal of becoming a master networker. Below is a plan for you to use as a guideline.

Networking plan:

1. Connect with segments of your network to talk about each of our goals.

2. Identify connections you would like to make with your targeted companies.

3. Reach out to dormant ties. They provide more valuable advice & more novel information compared to existing contacts.

4. Work networking into your daily life.

5. Join groups and sign up to attend in-person networking events.

6. Attends networking events with a friend to cover some more ground.

7. Share updates and thoughts of leadership regularly across your social media network.

8. Keep an eye for updates on your social media network and comment messages.

9. Use birthdays and holidays as an ice breaker and an opportunity to reconnect.

10. Setup blog or LinkedIn articles to publish on a regular basis.

Let me share with you a few examples that I have followed as per the above networking plan and to put it into perspective. I became a wizard in networking as per the assessment report and in my personal journey. I will give you real case examples:

Plan 1: I surrounded myself with mentors/coaches in my journey and always asked them for advice. One of the best mentors in my life – my wife. She is always there for me when I need her advice, listen to my problems at work, etc. She has guided me through many things in life, and we understand each other because she is my long-term partner. For example, she was who pushed me to do my MBA, which led me to my consultancy business and doing Toastmaster to meet my objectives. I've always wanted to make a Ted Talk and someday become an assistant professor and teach a class for a post-graduate university on a part-time basis.

Plan 2: I made a list of connections related to my industry on an excel sheet that I would like to target. I am now working toward making more connections. You need to plant seeds, as Ki told me, which is a never-ending journey. You also don't want to make the mistake of only asking for favours without offering something In return. It needs to be authentic and reciprocal. It is not about you, but what you can bring to the table for those connections. You need to think long-term.

Plan 3: I have reached out to my old friends and managed to secure a job and a two-year contract for my consultancy business.

Plan 4: I don't miss any networking events. I register for all either virtual or in-person. I stick a reminder to my daily calendar and follow it strictly. Once you miss one event, people will not invite you. As I mentioned, I was going to the British and American Embassy events, among other events that I was hosting.

Plan 5: I am quite active on WhatsApp and don't miss a chance to join a beneficial group. I know it is time-consuming, but you will collect more information and wait for an opportunity to arise. I can't even tell you how many professional WhatsApp groups I am in! There is no limit; the more, the better.

Plan 6: I usually go on my own to events as I am familiar and habitual of such an activity, and comfortable being surrounded with unfamiliar, new people.

Plan 7: I always post and publish articles on a frequent basis on my LinkedIn profile with market insight and analysis relevant to my industry; this creates engagement and communication with existing or new connections.

Plan 8: This goes without saying since I am super active on LinkedIn https://www.linkedin.com/in/ihab-tabbara/. I make sure that my voice is heard and write constructive messages with hashtags to increase the post reach.

Plan 9: I do use birthdays as an Ice breaker. However, now I just simply write a note and add someone to my profile to make it more personal. My conversion rate of being accepted is quite high, around 80 %, I'd say. I suppose this depends on your background, your profile, how active you are on social media, and, most importantly if your name has a buzz in the community.

Plan 10: I write my own articles and blogs on LinkedIn on a continuous basis.

In order to follow the above, you need a proper planning schedule, your priorities laid out, and a step by step guide. It takes time, but once you are in and give it your all, you will become a master like myself. I remember once going for a big interview for the position of CEO. I had to create a presentation for the board members. There were four people in that room, and two of them had heard of my name before and knew of me. That gave me an edge to break the ice and already put me at ease while presenting. I never heard back, but the timing was slightly off since COVID-19 came along, which may have caused a delay.

Once you have created your brand and understood its contributing factors, it is time to make yourself visible to the outside world. At the end of the day, you are doing this to get connections and business done. So, how are you going to build your visibility? This is the most fun part, one in which I have invested a lot of time.

Social Media:

This part is really the most intriguing since it will be a game-changer for you. How are you going to market yourself on social media? You don't want to go dark; otherwise, it will raise a question mark. You need to keep on advertising yourself and remember, visibility requires a lot of effort, and you need to adopt the mindset of a marketer.

Now, you will tell me that you are working as an employee and don't want to be noticed by your employer. "A disclaimer: you need to approach it carefully since employees should be aware of their workplace social media policy to avoid potential disputes with their employer." Trust me, the first step is always the most difficult, but soon you will be able to master it. There are three levels of social media behaviour that you should know about:

1. The passive: You are an observer and don't want to get your feet wet since you fear what other people might say about your post. You are constantly watching and learning.

2. The active: You contribute to the social media platform by liking and writing small comments on each post. That is not enough, but you are at least aware of the importance of diving in and letting your voice be heard.

3. The Proactive: You are the creator, and everything is under your fingertips. You are in control and know what you want.

A famous quote by Seth Godin is 'The easiest thing is to REACT, the second easiest thing is to RESPOND, but the hardest thing is to INITIATE.'

I will delve deeper into the proactive part and how you can become INFLUENTIAL on LinkedIn. You can either:

i. Comment on the posts of others.

ii. Share the posts you like.

iii. Publisher your own content.

Publishing is an art and can be categorized into the following four types:

i) Expert knowledge: You are the expert in your field and sector, and you know your stuff. An example would be industry whitepapers.

ii) Professional insight: You understand an industry and would like to share your insights related to your experience.

iii) An example would be a company's blog posts.

Point of view: You can comment and be heard just by adding a few points and observations. An example would be an opinion.

iv) Personal experience: You can share your overall personal experience as an example of a case study.

When you are writing posts, publishing articles, and case studies on a regular basis, the important part is to be consistent. You are getting likes and comments on your post, which will give you more views and visibility. It is a real rush when the post hit the 10k mark. Publishing content like articles will reinforce your personal brand and will give you access to conduct interviews and be part of keynote events or webinars. I became so good at it that I am now an influencer on LinkedIn. People were asking me to share their posts and to bring traffic into their blogs, events, etc.

To recap, I would like to share a diagram below, which I came across a year ago, as a guideline for you to be visible and elevate your personal brand. I will present a few examples that I have followed from the '22 ways' of getting visible to put it more into perspective. It is quite funny because now that I am writing this book, I just realized that I have subconsciously done 90 % of the points below. It is crazy how the mind plays tricks on you. You do things without really having the intention of doing it. I read this article a year ago without really focusing or prioritizing it.

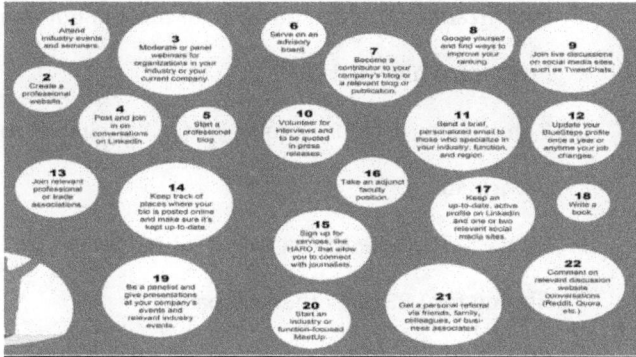

'22 ways'

1. I have completed it on many occasions, either virtually or in-person.

2. I have completed it with my 'Spectrum' Company.

3. I have organized and moderated eight webinars in a span of four months.

4. I am super active on LinkedIn.

5. I have my own blog on my website and LinkedIn profile.

6. I am now serving one of my clients on their advisory board.

7. People are now asking me for advice and use my key points on their blogs.

8. This is not yet done. It is all about search engine optimization. This is quite new for me, but one day I will learn how to do it.

9. I am joining webinars and getting the chance to participate.

10. I have volunteered for a couple of interviews and filming for LBS and other companies.

11. In one of my Webinars, I had to bring in three panellists. I sent ten personalized messages to invite them and become part of it. Five people replied, and I selected three of them.

12. Doing it.

13. Not yet.

14. I am keeping track of my bio on four different platforms.

15. Not yet.

16. I am working on getting an adjunct faculty position; it is part of my long-term goals and objectives.

17. Already doing it, and continually active. Even now, I have requested to stream live.

18. Doing it as we speak.

19. I always do presentations for my employees and my clients. I became very good. My next step is to be a panellist myself for a webinar.

20. Started my own consultancy.

21. I am getting referrals on my consultancy website for a project I have done.

22. I only comment on LinkedIn, Instagram, and Facebook for now.

So, go and get visible!

Key points:

My only advice here is to prioritize your life and objectives. You will carry your brand wherever you go. Strive to protect it well and to keep on evolving it as you go in each step of your life. I know it is a lot of work, but don't think of it in the manner as I did; you will be fine, and I am sure you will do quite well. Aim to stand out from the crowd and don't be a social loaf. "To lead the orchestra, one must stand apart from the crowd." Make sure you are trying to be visible and heard at all times, so people will remember you. You and only you hold the key to your success.

A famous quote by Jeff Bezos, "Your brand is what people say about you when you are not in the room," and another one from Steve Jobs, "There are no reasons to not follow your heart."

Those are two of my entrepreneurial idols.

Chapter 5: Transformation

'It is not the strongest of the species that survive, nor the most intelligent, but the one that is most adaptable to change.'

Charles Darwin

Now that you have gained a deeper understanding of branding yourself, I would like to take a moment to highlight some points made by Professor Kathleen O'Conner. I truly admire her work in the organizational behaviour field, and it is only now that I understand these theories she taught us during class. One of these theories touches on psychological and safety needs, which are the three ABC of basic needs, i.e., Autonomy, Belonging, and Competence (by Ryan and Deci's Self-determination Theory 2000), which help us make better and sound decisions in our life. We are the habits and rules we make for ourselves. It is up to us to break those roles by creating processes, goals, and constantly challenging ourselves.

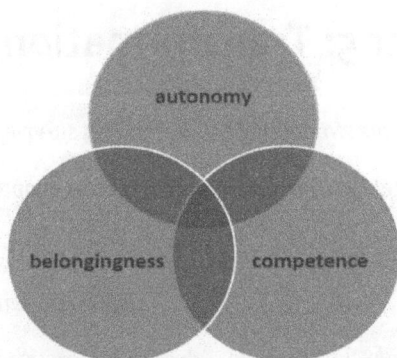

Ryan and Deci's *Self-Determination Theory* (2000)

- **Autonomy** is the desire to control one's behaviours and outcomes. However, the problem of employees is that they are locked down at home with their children or others who need their support. The solution would be for the employees to have more freedom in their workplace. Here are a couple of practices to consider:

  - Set clear goals and expectations.

  - Empower teams. Give them the freedom to experiment.

  - Stop micromanaging.

  - Allow clear times for reports submission.

- **Belonging** is the desire for a close relationship, to feel part of a group, free to express one's troubles. To tackle those issues, I would highlight the following points and practices:
  - Make it psychologically safe for one to ask for help and encourage volunteering to help.
  - Hold daily reflection meetings to catch up with your team.
  - Allocate time and space to talk with groups and individuals.
- **Competence** is the desire to play to one's strengths, demonstrate skills, and develop new ones. To apply in practice:
  - Encourage learning for researching relevant topics, online workshops, training, courses, and webinars.
  - Be forward-thinking and developing the ability to think outside the box in what the business might need.
  - Lead with trust.

In order to bring out the competence of an individual that exists in each of us, they need to feel free and connect with the ones around them. In many businesses that are target-oriented, company's tend to forget about their employees to a greater extent and focus on what the employees are expected to deliver, without caring for how the employees feel. You cannot disregard your employees like that, it will weaken your connection with them and will not be able to derive the required results.

Sit down and speak to them. Get to know them. How are they? What are their goals, desires, and expectations? What is it like for them at home? Anything they're going through, any burden you can help with? Don't sit and speak to them only when they are not delivering that gives them a selfish impression. You cannot create a feeling of belonging if you don't have such an environment. Setting deadlines are good, but not unrealistic ones. Doing this, you steal away their freedom and create a feeling of disrespect. Be fair to receive fair results.

My reasons for explaining the above points are that they will play a big role in your next career transition or transformation. You really need to think deeply about these points, because not everyone is willing to quit their job and go into their own adventure. If you feel you have some of the above symptoms, you can continue reading on and make your own journey and path in life.

The culture of the company where you work is also something to think about. What is the moral at the workplace or potential place of work? It is up to you to figure out the work culture environment that really fits you the best. Let me share my personal work experience during the 2006 period.

I had gained autonomy in my job since I was in control of the situation. At first, I will admit, I micro-managed, but once I found myself associated with the right team, I started to macro-manage. I simply implemented structures and policies, and it was up to my team to execute the projects. I just monitored and supervised the operation.

When it comes to belonging in the beginning, I was quite happy in the working environment I was in. The culture fitted me quite well. However, as time flew by, I felt like I did not belong there anymore. My talents and skills were not being appreciated, and to make matters worse, there was no room for growth. This is one of the reasons I applied for the MBA program at London Business School.

For Competence, we all have room to explore and grow. No one is truly knowledgeable or skilful in every aspect of life. The journey of knowledge never stops, even for me. I have finished my MBA, but I still take classes on specific topics on Coursera or even the Udemy platform. It is wise to always learn new things and understand the dynamics of the industry you find yourself in. Do not forget; people will always find the gap in the industry and attempt to disrupt it.

I would also like to highlight, again, the importance of having coaches/mentors in your life. For me, I find them very useful when it comes to getting advice. Having a second pair of eyes on something or a second opinion is always beneficial. Be honest with yourself, and admit that it does matter to you. You want to achieve your goals. However, you cannot just go out and pick the first mentor that comes across your path. You need to create a bond, a connection, and chemistry for the relationship to work for both of you. Do not forget that you are sharing intimate details of your life with this person; so, building trust is key. It is a long process, but, in the end, you will come out of it stronger, and it will be beneficial for you as a protégé.

Now that you have more of an understanding of your identity, you will need to explore it first before venturing forward and throwing yourself in the dark. This exploration is needed, or even your business plan might backfire on you. I really like the 'Working identity' book by Herminia Ibarra, also a professor at London Business School. She describes the following transition:

1. Ask who I might become first. Have a vision and plan in your mind. Explore any and all possibilities, talk to your friends, peers, and even family members. Get a sense from them and see how viable your idea is.

2. Test those assumptions and hypotheses. Try to see yourself in this new vision of you. I remember one of the assignments we had on our final journey at LBS was called 'Capstone.' We needed to prototype an individual. The idea for prototyping is to ask questions, create an experience, and reveal assumptions in order to have a sneak preview of the future that may lay ahead of us. Since one of my career paths was to reach the C-suite, I needed to put myself in his shoes and shadow

that person. I picked my uncle, who was the CEO of the biggest conglomerate company serving the construction industry in Saudi Arabia, managing over 200,000 employees. He has built an empire since the '80s, and he was a true entrepreneur and leader.

3. By following the two steps, you will be able to have a glance at the outcomes and see if there is a congruence of who we are and what we do. Basically, a congruence model is a balance between four aspects:

   I. Values & behaviours: Does the culture supports strategy?

   II. Organization & Structure: Does the structure support changes?

   III. People & skills: What type of leadership style is demonstrated?

   IV. Work

4. Of course, lastly, you need to keep updating your priorities and assumptions based on the outcomes.

Exploring Possible Selves
Asking Whom might I become?
What are the possiblities?

Grounding a
Deep Change
Updating priorities,
assumptions, and
self-conceptions

Lingering
between Identities
Testing possible selves,
both old and new

Outcomes
External change: Changing careers
Internal change: Greater congruence
between who we are and what we do

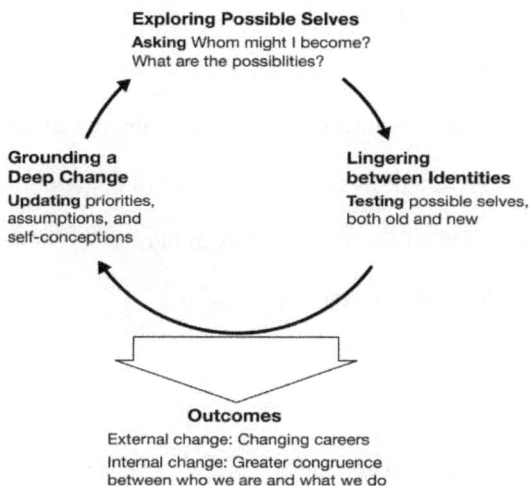

'*Working Identity' book – Herminia Ibarra'*

To tell you the truth, all this is all new to me as well. I was once like some of you reading this. I had no direction or sense of hope in life. I was not reading any books, nor was I visibly or even intellectually curious. My transformation started when I began my MBA journey and gave credit to my wife. She has always been supportive of me through all the challenges life has thrown our way. She was the one who pushed me to transform and start my MBA. My MBA has helped me get to where I am today since it has given me self-confidence, framework, structure, resources, and knowledge. I would not be where I am today without the MBA.

We can now delve into the transformation stage of your life. As a professor of Management at London Business School, Lynda Gratton explains in her book 'The new Long Life' the multiple stages of life.

1st stage: Education.

2nd stage: Work

3rd stage: Retirement

Here is my layout plan that I will elaborate more deeply on it:

Multiple stage plan graph

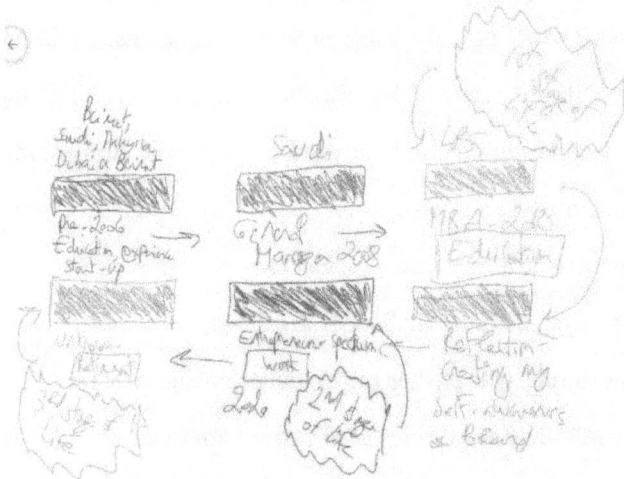

As you know by now, we all go through different stages of our lives. I, myself, have seen the ups and downs while travelling the world. I had good times and bad times. The question is, when and how should we make a transition? Can we afford it to take a leap of faith and venture out? Does the new company's work environment culture fit into ours? Are we able to take on the world by ourselves? There are so many unknown parameters, and only you and you alone can figure out the answers. In my book, I have tried to simplify and walk you through my life's journey and give you a guideline for a smooth transition. We all have our limitations, constraints, and hurdles in life. You need to find your own path and believe in yourself. I had a breakthrough in life at the age of forty-five. It is never too late to discover your identity. To emphasize more, I had my 'AHA' moment, which is the pivoting point of my 2nd stage of life.

I will try to recap and summarize my journey to highlight multiple stages.

- Pre-2006, I barely graduated from AUB with my BBA in four years. I had my first job in Saudi as a sales rep. I then move on to become a Sales &

Marketing Manager in Malaysia. Four years later, I went to work in Dubai as a Sales Manager. After I hit thirty, I decided to start my own venture with my wife in Beirut. Did it work out? No. There were a couple of reasons, one of which was the socio-political situation in Lebanon. In 2006, I moved back to Saudi Arabia to become the General Manager of a retail company selling building materials.

- In 2008, I worked for eleven years as a General Manager. I gained much exposure in my field and industry but had reached a plateau in my career back in 2016; hence I needed a change and new challenges.

- In 2018, stage one of my new life, I applied and joined the MBA program at LBS. I became the academic Rep; I have created an LBS Club for Alumni in Jeddah. I Learned, evolved, and became self-aware.

- Reflection time is where I started to read books, follow webinars, increase my curiosity, visibility, and work on my profile and brand identity on social media networks. I was participating in interviews and leads from recruiters. I landed an opportunity with my friend for a job in the same industry. I had my 'AHA' moment back when I was in London in September with my coach/ mentor Ki. It's hard to put this moment into words. I am sorry, but you will need to figure it out on your own since it is relevant to each individual's beliefs and mindset.

- In 2020 at age forty-six, stage two of my life, I have created my own retail consultancy company, Spectrum. I am happy with where I am today. I have the freedom to experiment and be myself. I have acquired a couple of clients in the last six months, which is an achievement for me, especially during COVID-19. I can say that I am proud of myself.

- Stage three in my life, a retirement plan, I have a couple of options which I am also working on to achieve, but only destiny can create my path for me. The first is for my kids to come and join my consultancy firm once they have graduated and acquired experience. The second is to be an assistant professor and educate students. The last one is to have a bookstore in a nice European mountain area to enjoy myself with Hana.

Key points:

Draw the multiple stages of your life and see in which stage you are at. Examine yourself and have a vision and a glance of the future. Prototype your assumption and measure the outcomes. Be open and receptive to your 'AHA' moments, maybe you already had it, and you were not aware of it. Albert Einstein found out that his theory of relativity was proven only after ten years of his theory being published.

Chapter 6: Entrepreneurship – Your leap of faith

'It's fine to celebrate success, but it is more important to heed the lessons of failure.'

Bill Gates

Let us now dive in and fast forward to the most important part of the book. Two questions I would like to cover here:

1) What is an entrepreneur?

2) How does one become an entrepreneur?

Part I
What is an entrepreneur?

Did you know that the word "entrepreneur" comes from the French verb 'entreprendre,' meaning "to undertake"? An entrepreneur is a person who pursues a venture to benefit from an opportunity, rather than working as an employee. Entrepreneurs play a key role in any economy. These are the people who have the skills and the necessary initiative to anticipate current and future needs, bringing good new ideas to the market.

I will illustrate a couple of examples of the biggest historical entrepreneurs for your reference:

Thomas Edison: Invented the light bulb in 1879.

Henry Ford: Invented automobile transportation in 1903.

Bill Gates: Founder of Microsoft, changed the course of personal computers in 1975.

Steve Jobs: Founder of Apple transformed computers and media devices in 1977.

Larry Page: Founder of Google, transformed online search and media in 1998.

Jeff Bezos: Founder of Amazon, transformed e-commerce in 2007.

Oprah Winfrey: Founder of her own TV talk show back in 2011.

Elon Musk: Founder of Tesla and SpaceX, changed the automobile sector into an electric vehicle back in 2015.

The question to ask is, do you consider yourself an entrepreneur and an iconic hero as per any of these people? The questions to ask yourself are:

1) Are you comfortable with public failure?

2) Do you like to sell?

3) Do you lack the skills to work on yourself?

Few people have the skills, personality, and characteristics that make up for being a successful entrepreneur. Below are the seven essential skills required to succeed:

1. Ambition.
2. Willingness to Learn. You always need to be up to date.
3. Ability to Listen. Communication is a two-way street.
4. Creativity. You must try new things to find what works best for you.
5. Confidence. Assert your opinion and belief.
6. Perseverance. Never give up. Remember that you only fail when you stop trying. Persistence is the key to success.
7. Courage and risk-taking. You need to take calculated risks along with a leap of faith.

The second question is, do you have what it takes to be an entrepreneur? Let me touch on Maslow's Hierarchy of Needs, "Pyramid theory." It is a theory of motivation which states that five categories of human needs that dictate an individual's behaviour, as explained in the graph below.

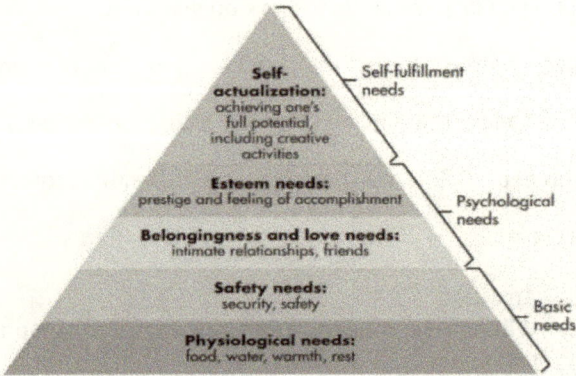

'Maslow's Hierarchy of Needs –

www.simplypsychologhy.org'

1. Physiological needs: It is the most basic of needs for any human's survival, such as food, water, clothing, and shelter. You need to address it before moving to the next step.

2. Safety needs: As the title mentions, we all need to feel safe and have financial security.

3. Love and belonging needs: We all need to feel a bond on a physical and emotional level with our family, friends, and peers. It is worth mentioning here also one of the ABC's of the self-determination theories of Ryan & Deci. At a company level, it is important to feel a connection

with the organization and culture to be productive at work

4. Esteem needs: Esteem can be broken into two parts: i) respect and acknowledgement from others ii) your own self-assessment and self-confidence.

5. Self- actualization needs: It is the fulfilment of your full potential as a person and redefining your talents. This is where your competence in Emotional Intelligence and your 'AHA' moment comes into play. It is a turning point for becoming an entrepreneur.

You need to figure out which stage you currently are in, in order to reach the top and become self-fulfilled. You need to start acting like a leader and step outside of your comfort and your psychological safety zone. For you to act like a leader, you must devote your time to bridge the gap you currently have. Such gaps could be engaging with new people, learning new skills, increase your curiosity, experiment, and take a risk for the sake of yourself and your dreams. Get involved in new projects, participate in extracurricular activities, and be adventurous. Basically, free your mind.

Maslow stated that only those who have met all of these needs could reach what we call self-actualization. The ability to reach your own true potential or be self-fulfilled. If this were true, no one would ever become an entrepreneur, to begin with.

True entrepreneurs are who sacrifice basic needs for their sheer passions. There are entrepreneurs who sleep on their office floors for several nights each week when the business was in a rapid mode of growth. Many entrepreneurs get so busy in their pursuit that they forget to eat or end up sacrificing healthy home cooking for whatever they can get quickly to sustain themselves. Entrepreneurs push themselves to their breaking point, enduring rather high levels of stress as they confront the unknown path up ahead.

Often the first act of towards being self-actualized is to throw away both safety and financial security with both your hands. Entrepreneurs often end up quitting their well-paying jobs, mortgage their houses and max out on their credit cards in attempts to manifest their dreams to reality. Then there's the obvious, most entrepreneurs find less time for their family and friends while pursuing their dreams. The needs of the business take over them completely. Entrepreneurs miss their kids' little league baseball games, drinks with friends and dinners with the family. Friends and family members will think the entrepreneur is crazy for giving up so much for their new enterprise. They may often question the entrepreneur's judgement in quitting their job and their sacrifices, risking financial security for the sake of ambition. Entrepreneurs we know of begin with self-actualization. They fulfil their dreams and desires with every pitch they make to investors, sale to a client or addition to their product and service being offered. They are one with their endeavours, and struggle is just a part of their joy.

One of the things I touched on in my previous chapter is networking. I would like to emphasize here, again, that without networking or connections, you would not be able to grow your business and become an entrepreneur. Effective networking will shape the flow of ideas, personnel, funding, and endorsement. It is like a spider web with an internal or external connection. You need to have strong ties within your network.

I want you to conduct a network audit exercise on yourself and see where you are at! It is a small exercise, and I guarantee you will find it quite enlightening.

Network Audit exercise

(This section is inspired by 'Act like a Leader, Think Like a Leader' Book by Herminia Ibarra)

Think of ten people with whom you have discussed matters of importance over the past few months. It can be anyone that matters to you, so as such, list their names below:

1. _____

2. _____

3. _____

4. _____

5. _____

6. _____

7. _____

8. _____

9. _____

10. _____

Now, you can list the top three strengths and weakness of having this connection in your network:

The main **Strengths** are:

1. _____

2. _____

3. _____

The main **Weaknesses** are:

1. _____

2. _____

3. _____

It's obvious, if you can't name 10 people that you've had a productive conversation with in the past few months, you lack connections, which means you are not meeting all the opportunities that await you. Hence, you are not capitalizing nor maximizing your potentiality. You can assess your connections depending on their strengths and weaknesses, how you can help them and they can help you, and so on.

There are many ways to expand your network. Among these ways: Attend conferences and meet at least three people. It is important to follow up with them over a coffee/tea catch up.

As you embark on your own destiny and path to entrepreneurship, it is vital to connect with the outside world. You need to act now and not be lazy, leaving things hanging and waiting for fate. Also, as I have mentioned to you earlier, you always need to surround yourself with a mentor, coach, or advisor. They are all there to help you, and they can further connect you with resources and networking.

Part II
How does one become an Entrepreneur?

Professor John Mullins, Associate Professor of Management at London Business School, in his book 'The New Business Road Test,' highlights the seven domains of an attractive opportunity. I recommend everyone to read this since my findings below are based on his book. It will put you on the right path to become an entrepreneur. It is the first step to take before venturing into your business.

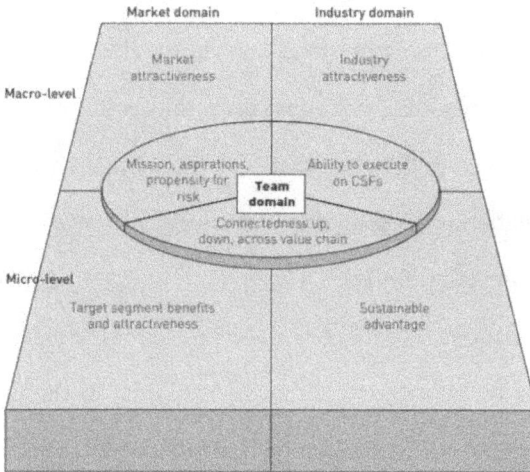

'The New Business Road Test' – 7th Domains, John Mullin book.'

To become a successful entrepreneur, you need to understand three crucial elements: market, industries, and people. This model offers a better toolkit for assessing and shaping market opportunities.

''A good opportunity can be found in not-so-attractive markets and industries. The market consists of buyers and not products, and the industry consist of sellers.'' – Mullins' quote

Let me elaborate more on each point of the seven domains. I divided them between the macro and micro-levels:

Macro-level:

You need to understand the market size by conducting relevant research, historical data, and publication on the market you wish to penetrate, i.e., size, the numbers of the population, geographic, demographic, age, gender, amongst other things.

A famous model I always like to use for the macro-level is the Five Forces of Porter, as exhibited in the diagram below that covers the market and industry attractiveness.

'Porter's Five Forces –
www.mindtools.com/pages/articles/newTMC_08.htm'

    a.   Competitive rivalry: How many players are there in the market? How do you differentiate from them? What is your added value?

    b.   Supplier power: How easy is it for customers to switch and substitute to different suppliers. Are you capturing a big market share with your unique product or service? Do you have a monopoly in the market? There are a lot of questions that need to be asked and answered.

c.   Buyer power: Is the customer sensitive to prices? The more customers you have, the more you control the market. If you have a fewer substitute, then the buyer power is weak since they have little choice.

d.   The threat of Substitute: Is your product unique, or can be easily substituted with an alternative product or solution?

e.   The threat of New Entry: Does your project require a high CAPEX? Which also suggest that the barriers to entry are also high. Can a rival enter the market easily due to particular regulation constraints?

1st Domain: Market attractiveness

You need to ask yourself questions to test your assumptions based on the research you will conduct before venturing out.

- What sort of business do you want?
- How large is the market you are seeing?
- How fast did it grow over the last few years?
- How quickly will it grow in the next six to twelve months?
- What factors, such as economical or socio-political, will affect the business?

All these questions require answering in the form of a structure to be able to have a glimpse into the future, understand and have the ability to take calculated risks.

2nd Domain: Industry attractiveness

- Again, I will give you a checklist of a few questions that you will need to analyse:

- What industry are you competing in? Example: Tech, FMCG, Retail, etc.

- Is the threat of entry high or low?

- How strong is the supplier power? High, Medium, or Low

- How about buyer power: High, Medium, or Low?

- How easy is it for customers to substitute your products or services? High, Medium, or Low?

- How intense is the rivalry? Is it price-driven or a product differentiation?

By using the Five forces of Porter, you can make your own judgment based on in-depth research and understanding. No one can give you the answers easily. You need to dig deep, reflect, and analyse. You are building a future for yourself, so please invest your time wisely. Do not take it lightly and have your own pre-determined assumption in your head. That is the trap that the majority of us fall into and is not easy to recover from.

Let me go back and give you an example of my first start-up in Lebanon back in 2003 with Asean Art. I made a lot of assumptions about customer needs and market requirements. It cost me a lot of money and time, which I can't recuperate now. The only thing I have learned is never to repeat the same mistake twice and, to make sure that I have all my facts and analysis right, and based on facts, I did not have an MBA, not the relevant knowledge at the time. That was a big step and learning curve for me. I am not saying you should have an MBA, but maybe have a partner who understands the market better than you or have some particular added value. Perhaps take a management course about entrepreneurship, or even read some good books. There are so many ways to do it, and whatever works best for you is the option you should pursue. If you do not have all the answers, figure it out at the macro-level, so at least you would have mitigated your own risk to a certain extent and have done your due diligence, ticking the relevant boxes to reach a point of confidence.

Micro-level:

You need to understand your customers' preferences. Is there a demand or need for the product or service you are offering? How large is the target demographic? We call this the minimum viable product, which I will come back to at a later stage.

Some entrepreneurs tend to only analyse the macro-level and ignore the micro-level. You need to look at the equation with a full spectrum to define your business plan before you begin planning. The devil is in the details.

3rd Domain: Target segments

There are three ways to define market segments:

- Who are your customers: Demographics (age, gender, income, etc.)?

- Where are your customers: Geographically?

- What is the general consumer behaviour?

Different markets require different needs, thereby, different solutions. Questions to ask yourself:

- What are your unique selling points? What are you resolving?

- Where is the evidence that a customer will buy from you? i.e., you can do a market survey.

- Does the data suggest that the market will grow?

4th Domain: Sustainability

This subject is quite an intriguing one for me. Basically, what is your competitive advantage that you are offering to your customers so that they will keep on buying or using your service? What if a disruptive model or a player steps into the industry? I remember a case study about 'Kodak' business. They used to be the # 1 player for developing photos from your analogue camera in the old days. Whenever you took a picture, people used to print them out for you. Soon they went bankrupt and eventually out of business. They did not follow the new trends, which were digital photos, and the people don't tend to print paper pictures any longer. All your pictures are now saved in the cloud or on your device. Basically, they missed their window of opportunity to follow the trend and adapt.

You need to be offering up to date products or services. If not, you will go out of business, as you'll have no sustainability. You could pivot your business at the appropriate moments to follow the trend and keep your market share.

Questions to ask yourself:

- Can your business develop and employ superior organizational process capabilities or resources?

- Is your business economically viable? In the sense that you will be able to sustain your cash flow in cases of downfall?

5th Domain: Dream

This is where you will need to have a mission, a vision, and an aspiration statement. If you strongly believe in something, you will make it happen and work. You are devoting your heart and mind to the business; failure is not an option. You are already in the Emotional Intelligence stage, where you are self-aware and self-confident that you will do your utmost best to succeed. You have dreams and goals, and you want to reach them by any means necessary. You will need to answer the following questions:

- Is your passion there? Do you really want to change the world?

- Do you want to build something or lead and manage?

- Are you willing to take the risk with no financial security and putting your own money on the table?

6th Domain: Execution

Do you have what it takes to execute and perform your task? Do you have the proper resources, skills, and mindset to become an entrepreneur? Just as in each sport, there are a few key attributes that separate the winners from the losers; the same is true for entrepreneurs... For example, I have spent the last six months setting up a company, working 24/7 after graduating from my MBA. I was devoted to my business, not missing out on any new skills to learn, taking online courses, reading books, webinars, networking events, planning, scheduling, and prioritizing my goals. Opportunity is out there, and you will get to look it in the eye, but not many times in life. It is like an athlete preparing for the Olympic trials. He spends four years getting one chance to qualify. If he misses it, he will have to wait another four years, and only God will know what might happen then. Age parameter, new gameplay, new rules, new regulations, or even records to be reached and broken. It is all about execution, timing, planning, hard work, and team collaboration.

7th Domain: Connectivity

You need to be able to connect the dots with all the stakeholders and the value chain. You hold the key to your success. You must be sharp, updated, on top of your business, and not be a pushover. You are in control, making sure you do not lose your mind. Use your EQ for social competence with empathy by developing and understanding others, and your communication and influence skills. Is it what holds the key? You should ask yourself these questions.

Now you need to put the seven domains into work and write your business plan as follows:

a) Business concept (Name, identity)

b) Business operation (How you will run your day to day operation?),

c) Business management (Who will run it?),

d) Financial analysis and forecast. We also call a Strategic Plan.

I will describe to you the ten-step guideline that I recommend for your business plan:

Step 1 Study the macro-level (market and industry attractiveness) and keep searching for opportunities.

Step 2 Business concept (dream.)

Step 3 Create a hypothesis and test your assumption.

Step 4 Generate an MVP (minimum viable product) by studying the micro-level (target segment & sustainability.)

Step 5 Business operations (execution.)

Step 6 Business management (connectivity.)

Step 7 Prioritize the MVP.

Step 8 Conduct tests and experiments.

Step 9 You can either pivot the business or reach your product-market fit.

Step 10 Financial analysis and forecast.

If you ask, how can we validate the MVP and test it? Well, we can do the following:

Interview: The rule of thumb is to have a minimum of three individuals who you have access to.

- **Surveys:** Make sure you ask the right questions.

- **Prototype:** Focus on physical products.

Another way for me to put it and to summarize all the above in layperson's terms is the seven simple steps for you to become an entrepreneur from my perceptive:

1. You must find the right business idea.

2. You must determine if you should get an education. It depends on which industry you are considering, either IT, automobile, etc.

3. Write down your business plan.

4. You need to find your target group/audience. Type, age, gender, and location.

5. Create a network. It is the key to any success, including the creation of close ties.

6. You must sell your idea to convince people to buy what it is you are selling.

7. You must find your market and scale-up.

The first step while developing your MVP, before weighing which features you need to build, is to ensure the product will align with your team's or your organization's strategic goals. What are those goals you'd set? Are you working toward a revenue digit in the next six months? Do you have limited resources at your disposal? These queries might affect whether now is even the time to start developing an MVP or not. Ask what purpose this minimum viable product is to serve. Will it attract new clients in a market adjacent to the market for your already existing sold products? If this happens to be one of your current business objectives, then this MVP plan may be strategically viable. But if your organization's priority is to continue on focusing on your core market, then you might need to perhaps shelve this idea and focus on an MVP designed to offer new functionality for your existing clientele.

Now that you have determined your MVP strategy aligning with your business objectives, you can start assessing the specific solutions you want your product to offer to users. These solutions, which you may write up in the form of user stories, epics, or features, do not represent the product's overall general vision but only subsets of that vision. Remember that you can develop only a small amount of functionality for your MVP, initially. Now that you have weighed the strategic elements mentioned above and settled on the limited functionality you've planned for your MVP, it is time to translate this into an action plan, you're your development. It is important to keep in mind the "V" in MVP. The product has to be viable. This means it must allow your customers to complete an entire task or a project, and it must also provide a high-quality user experience. An MVP cannot be an incomplete user interface with half-built tools and features. It has to be a working product that your company should be able to sell without much difficulty.

Airbnb: With little to no money to build a business, the founders of Airbnb used their own apartment to validate their idea, creating a market offering short-term, peer-to-peer rental housing service online. They created a minimalist type website, published photos and other details about their apartment, and found several paying guests almost immediately. For square: The location-based social network Foursquare began as just a one-feature offering MVP, with only check-ins and gamification rewards. It was not until they had validated the idea with an eager, growing user-base that the foursquare development team started to add recommendations, city guides, and other features. Now that you have read this chapter and my book, you can take a leap of faith in yourself since you have the answers and resources to mitigate your risks. Good Luck!

Are you ready to dive in?

Key points:
Be yourself, work hard to achieve your goals, do not give up, and follow the ten-step guidelines to success. I am

closing with my favourite entrepreneur Jack Ma, founder of Alibaba, who famously said, 'In carrying out e-commerce, the most important things are to keep doing what you are doing right now with passion, and to keep it up!'

Good Luck again in your career, and cheers to an amazing journey!

CONCLUSION

In essence, I have taken you through the different stages of my life and career. I have tried to inspire, share my wisdom, and explain to you how to reach your goals and become an entrepreneur. I will recap and summarize everything we have discussed.

Embrace every moment of your childhood and be self-sufficient.

Never give up during any studies you may partake in. No matter what major or field you go choose, you will succeed. Be resilient and open to change and learn new things during your personal and professional life. Build your self-confidence. Learn from your mistakes, and don't be afraid to take risks.

It is important to make decisions in life. If you are unhappy with your job, just quit or find another one. Don't wait for the opportunity to come to you; you must find it. Be proactive and hungry for success.

Trust yourself to succeed. Surround yourself with close friends, coaches, and mentors who think alike and are encouraging. They will guide you and put you on the right path. Don't be easily defeated. Be courageous. Think outside the box, step outside your comfort zone. Explore and experiment with new things. Be creative.

The future is waiting for you. Set goals and objectives. Plan ahead and put a structure in your life. Be good at time management. Make time to invest in your self-development and education. Learn new things by taking courses online, reading books and articles. Watch educational webinars, get an MBA or anything that you are passionate about. Everyone is unique. Take volunteering jobs, help the community, and you will see the reciprocity one day sooner than later.

Don't be afraid to throw yourself out there. Be visible on social media platforms, network, and connect with peers and friends. Make the first move!

You must know your strengths and weaknesses. Be self-aware and embrace it, building your own personal brand identity throughout your life and career. Envision multiple stages of your life and the many transformations in your life.

Never stop learning, the journey to seeking knowledge is a never-ending one. Build connections, use social media as a tool to increase your reach. Write blogs, share content, put your words out there to the world to see. Put yourself out there to capitalize on all opportunities. Don't shy away from communication, practice makes perfect. Build an extroverted mentality. Be a people's person, communication is key for creating and meeting opportunities. You have many options, you can be whatever you want.

You hold the key to your success. Either you want to grow and become the CEO of a company or become an entrepreneur. The choice is yours!

References

1. Marcus Buckingham: 'Stand out Report.' https://www.marcusbuckingham.com/

2. BlueSteps webinar & articles 'Global Guide to Personal Branding for executives' & 'The ultimate executive career guide.' www.bluesteps.com

3. Daniel Goleman book: 'Working with Emotional intelligence' - 1998

4. Herminia Ibarra book: 'Act Like a Leader and Think like a Leader' – 2015 & 'Working Identity' - 2003

5. John Mullin book: 'The new business road test' - 2013

6. Lynda Gratton book: 'The new long life' - 2020

Acknowledgments

Over the path of my forty-six-year life journey, I have made a lot of great friends, colleagues, peers, professionals, professors, coaches, and mentors that have inspired me to become a great leader. Each one has played a key role in my life. The book you have in your hands is the product of many's inspiration, and not simply mine.

First, I would like to dedicate this book to my lovely wife, mentor, and life partner, who has been by my side for the last twenty-eight years. She is my true inspiration, and without her, I would not be where I am today. She is my hero and has always pushed me outside of my comfort zone. Thank you, Hana; I love you, eternally!

My second inspiration is my coach, and mentor Ki Kuganesan. He has been the man behind the scenes during the last three years of my life. Thank you, Ki, for your time, effort, advice, and being next to me every step of the way, especially when I needed you the most.

Thank you, London Business School, for this wonderful journey and experience I have had over the last two years of my MBA studies. I want to express my gratitude to all the professors that have taught and share their insight, knowledge, and experience with us. I want to give a quick acknowledgement to Riza Jonsson, who belonged to the program office, and really has guided me through this tough journey at LBS and still continues to do so to this day. Thank you to Evie Boustantzi, President of the LBS Gulf Association, for giving me the chance to be the Club leader for LBS Jeddah Alumni. Thank you, Riz and Evie.

Here is the list of professors that I really admired:

Kathleen O'Connor from the Developing Effective Managers and Organizations course. Herminia Ibarra, with her inspirational books, Bryan Stroube, with the course of Developing Entrepreneurial Opportunities, Niro Sivanathan with the course of Negotiation & Bargaining. His teaching structure and scenarios that landed me my first consultancy job. Richard Jolly, with his Paths to Power course, Richard Hytner with Creativity in Business course, Michael Jacobides with the Managing Corporate Turnarounds course, who has opened my eyes to a different spectrum. David Myatt with Managerial Economics course, Olenka Kacperczyk with Strategic Management course, John

Mullins & Lynda Gratton with their inspirational books. Thank you to everyone!!!

To my coaches and mentors, thank you, everyone, for being my friend. Rula Kurban a true friend and a career advisor. Roisin O'Kane, my executive coach during the MBA, Karima Tani, my public speaking mentor.

To my LBS friends and classmates, thank you all for your vote of confidence, and thank you for giving me the chance to be your academic representative during this MBA program; and also enabling me to learn from your experience. You have truly opened a new door for me: Salah Fayad, Ahmed Remayyed, Dani Hijazi, Hania Qatafi, Hazem Adawi, Lama Khalil, Omnia Kelig, Yousuf Al Yousuf, Ayesha Jahangir, Ali Zainal, Tariq Siddique, Mohammed Albalaihed, Vijya Kallam, Felice Galati, Tala Raad, Sultan Al - Nabulsi, Ibrahim Almohaimede, Natalie Pietrobon, Hisham Al Halabi, Khaled Maseeh, Ramzi Qannati, Mohammed Al Nefeily, Qaiz Qureshi, Sami Arwardi, Yazeed Alyahya, and finally Salman AliReza who is also now my partner at Spectrum and the person who inspired me to choose the title of this book.

To my close friends and colleagues, thank you for being with me on this journey. Peter Sarkis, my tennis partner, Nader Sfeir, Toni Akiki, Omar Sawwaf, my cousin who has been with me through the up and downs. Tarek Tabbara also my cousin, Mohammed Shehab, Mazen Maroun, Mohammed Khaled, Rupert Armes my ex-employee, Fadi Sukkar my ex-employee, Bassam Jabi my first boss, and finally Karim Salamoun, who really inspired me to start writing a book, who is also my finance freelance and whizz partner.

A special thank you to my uncle, Mutaz Sawwaf, for giving me this career chance over the last twenty-two years, from the good times to the bad times.

Finally, to my family: My dad, Ahmad Tabbara, who is also my inspiration and my hero. My mom, Rima, for giving birth to me, my brother Toufic, my sister Rania, and my children Ryan, Jade, and Lynn. They are my life and a gift from God. Thank you all, and I love you from the bottom of my heart.

About the Author

Ihab is a Managing Partner at Spectrum, a retail consultancy firm, and is a certified executive coach. He has accumulated more than 22 years of first-hand experience in running a successful multi-site operation in the retail industry.

Having gained his MBA from London Business School in 2019 with a student award and with his entrepreneurial mindset and creative thinking, Ihab went onto specializing in strategic planning and marketing.

Having established and managed a retail business from just an idea to becoming its General Manager, he has been actively involved in all aspects of the retail industry, from supply chain management and business development to strategic planning and leadership.

As part of his previous job responsibility at Roots Group Arabia from 2006 till 2019, he has successfully grown the business to 40 showrooms, managing 140 employees, operating within the MENA region, and trading in Saudi Arabia, Lebanon, Egypt, Syria, and the UAE.

Ihab started his career in executive sales for a period of two years in Jeddah, Saudi Arabia, in 1996. He was then promoted and worked for four years in Kuala Lumpur, Malaysia as a Sales and Marketing Manager back in 1998. Further to that, he was reallocated to work in Dubai, UAE as a Sales Manager for a year in 2002.

Eventually, I had decided to start his own retail business in Beirut, Lebanon, in 2003. Concerning his career path, Ihab has been fiercely determined with passion and result oriented.

During his free time, Ihab has created an Alumni Chapter for London Business School in 2019, comprising over 100 members, where he organizes monthly social gatherings and quarterly keynote speaking events. On top of that, he is a moderator, event organizer, and public speaker.

Ihab is married with three children and enjoys travelling with his family. He enjoys sports, running, and tennis. He is a very proud father to his two sons, who is currently studying Engineering.

This is the success story of the author Ihab Tabbara along with key lessons and thoughts to help his readers succeed in life. The book speaks about finding yourself, building connections, taking risks and never giving up. The authors versatile life experiences all over the world have helped shape him into the man that he is today.

The book takes a dive in the concept of emotional intelligence and how it effects our day to day lives. It speaks about time management, utilizing social media and significant entrepreneurial terms and processes that can really have an impact on those seeking their dreams and desires.

This book is a must read for anyone who is looking to develop themselves, perhaps building a brand, understanding the world from a versatile scope of view, and even people who want to read a good knowledgeable success story.

The book offers some great insight in leadership qualities, how to adapt to them and become a better version of yourself, the value of constantly working on yourself and adapting to new trends and standards, all the while discussing the authors journey in life.

"Your brand is what people say about you when you are not in the room" - Jeff Bezos

About the Author

Ihab Tabbara is a consultant and a coach who has gained his MBA from London Business School. With his entrepreneurial and creative thinking mindset, he went onto specializing in strategic planning and marketing. He is now the Managing Partner at Spectrum, a retail consultancy firm, after having accumulated over 22 years of first-hand experience in running a successful multi-site operation in the retail industry.

www.ingramcontent.com/pod-product-compliance
Lightning Source LLC
LaVergne TN
LVHW091252080426
835510LV00007B/225